Feluda

Boria Majumdar, a Rhodes scholar, went to the University of Oxford. His doctorate was published as *Twenty-Two Yards to Freedom: A Social History of Indian Cricket*. He has taught at the universities of Chicago, Toronto and La Trobe, where he was the first distinguished visiting fellow in 2005. He was also a visiting fellow at Trinity College, University of Cambridge, in 2009. He is currently senior research fellow at the University of Central Lancashire and consulting editor, sports, at the India Today Group.

Boria is the co-author of Sachin Tendulkar's autobiography *Playing It My Way*, and is one of India's leading sports scholars and journalists. Some of his other books include *Olympics: The India Story, Goalless: The Story of a Unique Footballing Nation* and *The Illustrated History of Indian Cricket*.

*For Aisha (Teeny) who I am sure will grow up
to be a huge Feluda fan*

Feluda @ 50

Curated and Edited by

BORIA MAJUMDAR

HarperCollins *Publishers* India

First published in India in 2016 by
HarperCollins *Publishers* India

Anthology copyright © HarperCollins *Publishers* India 2016
Copyright for individual essays rests with the contributors
Photographs copyright © Society for the Preservation of
Satyajit Ray Archives 2016

P-ISBN for HB edition: 978-93-5177-790-8
P-ISBN for PB edition: 978-93-5136-578-5
E-ISBN: 978-93-5136-579-2

2 4 6 8 10 9 7 5 3 1

Boria Majumdar asserts the moral right
to be identified as the editor of this work.

HarperCollins *Publishers*
A-75, Sector 57, Noida, Uttar Pradesh 201301, India
1 London Bridge Street, London, SE1 9GF, United Kingdom
Hazelton Lanes, 55 Avenue Road, Suite 2900, Toronto, Ontario M5R 3L2
and 1995 Markham Road, Scarborough, Ontario M1B 5M8, Canada
25 Ryde Road, Pymble, Sydney, NSW 2073, Australia
195 Broadway, New York, NY 10007, USA

Typeset in 12/15 Adobe Garamond
By Saanvi Graphics Noida

Printed and bound at
Replika Press Pvt. Ltd.

Contents

Part One

রাজেনবাবুকে রোজ বিকেলে ম্যাল-এ আসতে দেখি। মাথার চুল সব পাকা, গায়ের রং ফরসা, মুখের ভাব হাসিখুশি। পুরোনো নেপালি আর তিব্বতী জিনিসটিনিসের যে দোকানটা আছে, সেটায় কিছুক্ষণ কাটিয়ে বাইরে এসে বেঞ্চিতে আধঘন্টার মত বসে সন্ধে হব হব হলে জালাপাহাড়ে বাড়ি ফিরে যান। আমি আবার একদিন ওঁর পেছন পেছন গিয়ে ওঁর বাড়িটাও দেখে এসেছি। গেটের কাছাকাছি যখন পৌঁছেছি, হঠাৎ আমার দিকে ফিরে জিগ্যেস করলেন, 'কে হে তুমি, পেছু নিয়েছ?' আমি বললাম, 'আমার নাম তপেশরঞ্জন দত্ত।' 'তবে এই নাও লজঞ্চুস' বলে পকেট থেকে সত্যিই একটা লেমনড্রপ বার করে আমায় দিলেন, আর দিয়ে বললেন, 'একদিন সকালে এসো না আমার বাড়িতে—অনেক মুখোশ আছে, দেখাবো।'

সেই রাজেন বাবুর যে এমন বিপদ ঘটতে পারে তা কেউ বিশ্বাস করবে?

ফেলুদাকে কথাটা বলতেই সে খ্যাক খ্যাক করে উঠল।

'পাকামো করিসনে। কার কী করে বিপদ ঘটবে না-ঘটবে সেটা কি মানুষকে দেখলে বোঝা যায়?'

Decoding Feluda: What Makes the Fifty-year-old Tick?

Boria Majumdar

There is no gainsaying the influence of the West on our cultural imagination. We continue to admire their universities, their libraries and sense of history, architecture, beautified parks and most of all their opulence. We have fashioned our shopping malls – synonymous with development in most Indian cities – on the Western model and follow Hollywood religiously. The Oscars and the BAFTA are more credible than our own film awards and, a refurbished Eden Gardens and a powerful Indian cricket board notwithstanding, Lord's is still the Mecca of cricket with its long-standing legacy and two-hundred-year-old tradition. There are more Indians who now follow Leo Messi and Cristiano Ronaldo than there are who follow Mohun Bagan, East Bengal, Kerala Blasters and Delhi Dynamos. It is more about quality than sentiment. The English Premier League (EPL), the most competitive football league in the world, has a huge viewership in India and many of the leading EPL clubs are looking at the huge Indian market to add to their support base. In an increasingly globalized world, we are citizens of cosmopolitan international cities with seemingly unrestricted choice.

Yet, the one count where the Bengali looks homeward is in our allegiance to literary sleuths. Not that biggies from around the world are absent from our bookshelves. From the father of all detectives, Sherlock Holmes, to Agatha Christie's little Belgian superman, Hercule Poirot, to the quintessentially British Inspector Morse, or the Swedish Kurt Wallander – they are all detectives with impeccable credentials. For us, however, these men were never the primary draw. All we ever wanted to be was Feluda. While there are those who hold out for Byomkesh, Sharadindu Bandyopadhyay's creation is no competition for the quintessentially Bengali brand in the world detective supermarket: Feluda. Every Bengali, young and old, is a Feluda fan. We like his looks, his mannerisms, his wit, his tongue-in-cheek humour and finally his ability to solve one mystery after another despite being pitted against the most dangerous of criminals. We like that he is honest and intelligent, agile and courageous. We like it that Feluda is never outmanoeuvred and even when he is in a tight spot, manages to come up with the most innovative of plans to get himself and his associates, Topshe and Lalmohan-babu, out of trouble. For example, in *Badshahi Angti* when Bonbihari Sarkar and his assistant Ganesh Guha try to confine Feluda and Topshe in the jungle house and set the python free, Feluda at the very last minute throws a box of pepper at them. It has instant impact and the two reprobates are taught a serious lesson. Again, in *Bombaiyer Bombete*, Feluda plays a masterstroke by taking Victor Perumal into confidence and it is Victor's timely intervention in the train sequence that helps him nab the smuggler-turned-producer Gopinath Gorey. Also, Feluda too makes mistakes but has the courage to own up to them and wiggle out of tight situations caused by these mistakes. One such was when he says in *Baksha*

Rahasya that the craving to give an autograph is no less than the craving to take one. It is this lure, Feluda's keenness to sign an autograph, that allows the criminal to come to his room at the Janpath Hotel in Delhi and steal the blue briefcase.

To me, Feluda is also a powerful link to my childhood and youth. It was the *Feluda Samagra* I picked up to give me company on my way back from Oxford on 1 October 2000 when I had to rush back to Kolkata for my father's last rites. I may not have read a single word then, but I held the book through that entire flight back home. It was the only book that I could think of reading on a fateful journey like that, something that best sums up my personal fondness for the man. Again, it was Feluda who stayed with me when I made it back to Oxford in January 2001, nervous and apprehensive having missed a term. Feluda is an inspiration, and suffice it to say I am not alone in saying so. There are millions of Indians who just love him and his traits.

There are good reasons for why Feluda speaks to me and the legions of his fans in this way.

Take Sherlock Holmes for a study in contrast. Brilliant and agile as he may be, his many quirks and mood swings are alienating. His experiments on the beautiful Saint Bernard, Gladstone, integral to the new Guy Ritchie Holmes movies, don't often go down well with dog lovers like me. And more recently, Holmes has been subjected to multiple experiments, which have not often been well received by the discerning viewer. *Elementary*, the Holmes adaptation with Johnny Lee Miller starring as Holmes and Lucy Liu as Dr Watson, is well crafted but many have problems in accepting Dr Watson as a woman. Also, while there are takers for Lee Miller as Holmes, questions have been asked if he has actually ended up doing disservice to the character. Tim Martin, writing for the *Daily Telegraph*, has this to say about Lee Miller as Sherlock: 'An example of how not to do it (Sherlock Holmes) came with *Elementary*, the other contemporary Sherlock drama that features Jonny Lee Miller as Holmes fresh out of drug rehab and living with Lucy Liu's Dr Watson. The writers of *Elementary* pay lip service to the alien side of Holmes, but Miller offers a performance devoid of human warmth, all gleaming teeth and swivel-eyed self-interest.'

He goes on to say that 'Jeremy Brett offered what many consider the defining performance in many TV productions of the Eighties and early Nineties, his majestic stately face and beautifully modulated tones contrasting with a gangling twitchy physicality and white-hot outbursts of fury. Brett, who suffered from bipolar disorder, later reported having recurring nightmares about Holmes, whom he referred to as "the man without a heart" and, later, as "You Know Who".'

Hercule Poirot on the other hand is a dandy and is fond of the real luxuries of life. He stays in the best of five-star hotels and loves exotic food, things the middle-class Indian cannot identify with. He is an immaculately dressed snob. While he is chivalrous and respectful of women, he is often dismissive of Captain Hastings, his sidekick. So while he is admired, Poirot will forever remain the exotic Belgian, one we will never aspire to be.

John J. O'Connor, writing for the *New York Times* in December 1996, had summed up Poirot nicely: 'No one is likely to argue that Christie and Poirot are for the ages, but for the moment and, thanks to these adaptations (done for television with David Suchet as Poirot), for at least the next decade or two, they are great fun. Mr Suchet's Poirot is one of those deliciously precise depictions ... that have brought steady distinction to "Mystery" over the years ... With his delicate manners and dandy wardrobe, Poirot could easily seem a merely ridiculous figure, overly smug about the ability of his "little gray cells" to solve any crime tossed their way.'

Miss Marple is the very opposite of Poirot. She is a sharply intelligent, amiable village lady, but for youthful readers who see themselves in the protagonist's shoes, she is just too old to be a detective.

Inspector Morse, of course, is an alcoholic. Now, you might be brilliant, but you can't be a Bengali idol if you are an alcoholic. Yes, he drives a beautiful red Jaguar and fancies his single malt, but that only means Morse can never be the average Indian that Feluda personified. With his Oxford and his Wagner and the opera, and the occasional rudeness with his underlings, he is more than once removed from us. His mood swings are difficult to deal with, and even Lewis, his associate and friend, thinks he's a handful. Not that much of an ideal to aspire to then?

And in Wallander we see a work-obsessed detective who has no family to go back to in the evenings. His daughter Linda might love him, but she does not live with him. Wallander's alcoholism, which has only grown over the years, has landed him in trouble on a number of occasions and he too suffers from serious mood swings. A bitter man who finds it difficult to concentrate for long periods, his methods of policing are unconventional – and there is a veiled disregard for the law apparent in it. So, no, Wallander is no Feluda.

One could go on and on for many a famous detective has won over the Bengali reader.

But let's move on to Prodosh C. Mitter. He is tall and handsome, well read and well behaved, and is a man of the world – bhadro in every sense. Equally, he is at ease doing a kung fu stunt and trying the exotic Chinese cuisine in Hong Kong. Yes, he is pensive on occasions, but never rude to Lalmohan-babu or Topshe. He still uses public transport. The very thought of Feluda using a swanky smartphone and smoking a cigar is ridiculous. A Charminar man, Feluda, unmarried as he is, has the highest regard for family. That he stays with Topshe's parents, despite working in a bank for five years, and nearing thirty is an indication of his mindset and his regard for middle-class values.

Also, in Feluda we find the archetypal Bengali foodie. From chanachur to his other culinary tastes, be it the traditional mangshor jhol or mishti or the more exotic oriental cuisine in Hong Kong, Ray's immortal Rajani Sen Road resident has a genuine curiosity about food. For example, in *Chhinnamastar Abhishap*, Feluda does give in to Lalmohan-babu's request and visits the Great Majestic Circus, but only after he has finished his chicken curry and arhar dal lunch, cooked by the chowkidar's wife in Hazaribagh. Again, in the film rendition of *Joi Baba Felunath*, the second of Satyajit Ray's classic Feluda films, Feluda thoroughly enjoys his fish curry for lunch, something he mentions to Mr Chakraborty, the hotel manager, before going on to add, '*Kashi te ato bhalo machh pawa jay jantam na toh.*' (I wasn't aware that you get such good-quality fish in Kashi.) On being informed by Mr Chakraborty that getting good-quality fish isn't easy, Feluda, while licking his fingers, suggests, '*Chharben na, antata amra je kata din achhi.*' (Don't leave it, at least for the few days that we are here.) In the most recent film adaptation, *Badshahi Angti*, which released in December 2014, Sandip Ray has added a scene where Feluda is seen enjoying the famous kakori and galouti kebabs in Lucknow – a departure from the original that no Feluda fan is unhappy with.

What has added much to the Feluda cult is how cinema, stories and novellas all combine and meld, making it impossible to talk only about the written word. For example, any talk on *Sonar Kella* inevitably combines the novel and the film, with the written word and the visual appeal blending into one composite whole. Made by the same person who created the character, *Sonar Kella* and *Joi Baba Felunath* have both attained cult status as films and continue to be enjoyed by discerning Bengali audiences across the world.

Finally, we love Feluda because he is one of us. He is the Bengali Harry Potter and most importantly, we could be him too. Whether or not he is the best detective is immaterial because to most Bengalis he is much more than a sleuth.

The Magic of Lalmohan-babu

Interestingly enough then, Prodosh C. Mitter is probably not the most loved character in the Feluda universe. That particular award must go to Lalmohan-babu. Short, stocky, witty and talented, Lalmohan-babu is a writer of crime stories. The alliterative titles of his novels, written under the nom de plume of Jatayu, make their way into every kind of Bengali banter. He is vibrant and entertaining, but also unpredictable and resourceful. His use of the boomerang in *Baksha Rahasya* or his use of the 'jap jantra' in *Joto Kando Kathmandute* was pure genius. It is this streak of brilliance that sets him apart from the somewhat boring Ajit in the Byomkesh adventures, or the enthusiastic Arthur Hastings, or even the serious Dr Watson. Even Sergeant Lewis in the Inspector Morse stories, one of my favourite sidekicks, is no match for the man from Garpar in north Kolkata. None of those other associates could have said, 'one of the innumerable dacoits in this dacoit-infested country', or 'hnayes' (combining 'hna' and 'yes'). Only Lalmohan-babu would ask the owner of the Great Majestic Circus, '*Sher toh bhaga* but how?' His lovability and eccentricity are heightened by an intelligence he does not wear on his sleeve.

Sandip Ray chose to film *Badshahi Angti* – a story that predates Lalmohan-babu's appearance in the Feluda universe – in 2014 because he is yet to find the new Lalmohan-babu. The actor Santosh Dutta was the first to play him, in *Sonar Kella*, and then again in *Joi Baba Felunath*. Although he has acted in other, equally iconic Satyajit Ray movies, it is as Jatayu that he is best remembered. Actors who have played the character after Dutta admit to his shadow looming over them. Lalmohan-babu is witty, not foolish; he is a little spaced out, not dumb – distinctions that are difficult to portray on screen. This is what Sandip Ray has to say about Dutta: 'Not always do you get a character who forces the creator to change the illustration of the character in the next novel. Hardly has such a thing happened in world literature. It happened with Santosh Dutta as Lalmohan-babu. Baba had to change the very illustration of the character after Santosh Dutta played Lalmohan-babu in *Sonar Kella*. In the original novel, Lalmohan-babu is only three-and-a-half years older than Feluda. But with Santosh Dutta taking over, the age difference becomes a lot more.'

My own association with Lalmohan-babu too started with *Sonar Kella*, which I first read and then watched as a child. Here was a mystery novel writer who learnt a lot from Feluda, who never failed to acknowledge how talented and bright Feluda was and yet was entirely his own person. Feluda with all his brilliance was never able to overshadow Lalmohan-babu in the manner of the Poirot–Hastings or Holmes–Watson relationships. And so, without Lalmohan-babu playing the role of the art professor to perfection, there is no *Kailashe Kelenkari*. Much to my delight, he took to calling Topshe 'Bhuto' in that capacity. Again, without Lalmohan-babu, there would be no *Royal Bengal Rahasya* (his book kick-starts the adventure). By Feluda's own admission, 'No one has ever managed to hang on a tree trunk after losing consciousness,' like Jatayu does in *Royal Bengal Rahasya*.

He is equally central to *Joi Baba Felunath*. In the standout scene from the movie – where Lalmohan-babu is being tormented by Maganlal Meghraj – Santosh Dutta balances the comic and the horrific with exquisite ease. It is the resulting sense of helplessness that literally pushes Feluda to the brink. The scene is crucial in one other way: that Lalmohan-babu, despite his terror, calmly gets up and stands in front of the near-blind knife thrower, Arjun, is a clear demonstration of his commitment to Feluda and Topshe, and of his courage. Despite his elevated pulse rate (ninety-seven, as all fans of the movie will remember) in the aftermath of the knife-throwing ordeal, Lalmohan-babu tells Feluda, '*Apni tadanta chaliye jan, Felu-babu, ami apnar pashe achhi.*' (You carry on with the investigation, Felu-babu, I am with you.) That Maganlal had left a lasting impression on Jatayu is evident in future novels, and all of this adds to the aura of the character. From the very start of the scene, Santosh Dutta is at his finest. By trying to suggest he isn't hungry, he does his best to ensure Maganlal isn't able to feed them something spurious. Only when he sees Feluda having the sharbat does Lalmohan-babu feel encouraged to sip it. And when Maganlal calls Arjun to demonstrate his art, Lalmohan-babu is just brilliant. He very slowly says, '*Ek* minute', and then gradually starts to open his watch and hand it over to Topshe. Each movement of his, slow and laboured, adds to the occasion. He takes out his notepad, pen and purse and very slowly walks up to Topshe to leave these belongings on the table. His expressions are such that the viewer knows what he is thinking: that he may well die in the bargain. With 'haribol...' playing in the background, the sequence has an incredible impact on the audience. While feeling the tension, Lalmohan-babu does manage to rile Maganlal by his tactics of trying to delay the inevitable.

From the very moment he makes Feluda's acquaintance in *Sonar Kella*, Lalmohan-babu has been with Felu and Topshe through the good and bad. Speaking of that story, it wouldn't be wrong to suggest that Santosh Dutta (inseparable in the Bengali mind from the character) is central to the film's transformation into a classic. His body movements, facial expressions, postures and dialogue delivery are the very embodiment of Lalmohan-babu to every Bengali.

Satyajit Ray has endowed Jatayu with sterling qualities. He is a man of principle, which is established right in the beginning, when he says to Feluda, 'Share-*e jabo kintu*.' (We'll share the taxi fare.) At no time in *Sonar Kella* does he leave Feluda, then a new acquaintance, in a spot of bother and walk away.

Lalmohan-babu is not a sidekick, but a co-hero. He is central to the Feluda oeuvre and therein lies his uniqueness in the genre of mystery stories globally. The only other assistant to the sleuth that I can readily think of with this level of authority is Captain Haddock in the Tintin comics. Not a bad comparison, come to think of it, given that Haddock is probably the most loved character in that series. The unassailable popularity of Feluda is also in part due to the standout charisma of Lalmohan-babu, the prototypical Bengali. His sweet tooth and love of good tea, and his profession of course, all beautifully define the Bengali middle-class ethos. Ray, needless to add, is a past master at capturing that.

Also, Lalmohan-babu has a flamboyant streak that nicely sets off Feluda's pragmatism. He buys a Japanese horn for his car that Feluda begins to detest, tailors an orange suit in Hong Kong in the little time that they are there and picks up a colourful Nepali cap in Kathmandu. His choice of weaponry, bhojali (dagger) in *Sonar Kella*, smoke bomb in *Kailashe Kelenkari*, boomerang in *Baksha Rahasya* all point to his penchant for drama. The names of his novels, *Saharay Shiharan* and *Hondurase Hahakar* are further proof of this. Behind his flamboyance, however, he is the archetypal Bengali middle-class bhadrolok. Who else would wear a 'monkey cap' in Hazaribagh – as Lalmohan-babu so daringly does in *Chinnamastar Abhishap* – citing the possibility of catching a cold.

There are two ancillary points that shore up the Lalmohan-babu charisma. When Feluda suggests, in *Baksha Rahasya*, that it is expensive to travel to Shimla, Lalmohan-babu very politely reminds him that he has twenty-seven bestselling novels to his credit. There is a veiled assertion (meant without any malice) that, despite all of Feluda's success, Lalmohan-babu still earns more. Watson and Hastings are unlikely to make such an assertion. Again, it is Lalmohan-babu's car that the trio always uses, something Feluda is totally comfortable with. Jatayu often shares a room with Feluda and Topshe when they travel. He is more family member than friend, and that's what makes the bonding between the three special. Their repartee, from the very beginning, is affectionate and indulgent. In *Sonar Kella* (the movie), when Jatayu seeks permission to ask a question on the way to Jaisalmer, all Feluda says is, sure.

> **Jatayu:** *Ut niye proshno kora cholbe?* (Is asking a question on camels permitted?)
>
> **Feluda:** *Cholbe.* (Yes, it is.)
>
> **Jatayu:** *Uter khadya ki?* (What do camels eat?)
>
> **Feluda:** *Pradhanata kanta jhop.* (Mainly thorny bushes.)
>
> **Jatayu:** *Ut ki kanta bechhe khay?* (Do they separate out the thorns when they eat?)

That's Lalmohan-babu for you: much more than an associate. He is a star, a true Bengali icon.

Feluda's Villains: From Dr Hazra to Maganlal Meghraj

What makes Feluda tick? What explains his popularity? To probe deeper into this, I must talk about the villains. Feluda is pitted

against adversaries whose brilliance often threatens to outshine
his own. The villains are superstars in their own right. They bring
the best out in Feluda too – and that might be one clue to why
our man from Rajani Sen Road remains so compelling from one
generation to the next, for five decades.

Of all the villains, Maganlal Meghraj has a special place, no
doubt in part because of the character played to perfection by
the legendary Utpal Dutta in Satyajit Ray's *Joi Baba Felunath*. In
both the book and the movie, it is evident from the get-go – when
Maganlal comes to meet Machhli Baba – that there is something
special about him. In the film, he just walks past Feluda and
his team, his face indifferent. Then we see him, sitting in front
of the baba, intently listening to Reba Muhuri sing '*Mohe lage
lagana*'; his face has an element of ruthlessness even in repose.
The quiet menace of the man only grows through the movie.
As I said earlier, one of the best scenes in it is the humiliation
of Lalmohan-babu, and how it brings everything to a head.
Maganlal had initially tried to bribe and intimidate Feluda
into stopping the investigation. It is only when Feluda turns
aggressive in his attempt to stop the bullying of Lalmohan-babu
does Maganlal start to show his true colours. Even as he screams
at the servant who fired the pistol at Feluda, Maganlal adds that
he would deduct the cost of the broken flower vase from the
man's salary. Yet, that parsimoniousness is gone as he watches
the skilful Arjun at his knife throwing. He respects talent, even
in an enemy: evident when he observes that Feluda is endowed
with an extraordinary brain. But it is his domain – and even
Prodosh Mitter is rendered powerless in front of Maganlal for the
time being. Feluda's helplessness and vulnerability in that scene
are crucial to the pay-off that the viewer gets from the eventual
revenge. I believe it also holds yet another key to what endeared
Feluda to his scores of fans.

Maganlal is no ordinary villain and that is the real point. Moving base to Kathmandu comes easy to him and he has the unique ability to laugh at himself. His ability to joke about his own weird behaviour after he is forced to consume the cube of LSD in jail in Kathmandu is just extraordinary.

Clearly the standout villain in the Feluda oeuvre, he is one of those villains in the pantheon of Indian cinema who will continue to have universal appeal. Barring *Sholay's* Gabbar Singh played by Amjad Khan, and Mogambo, the larger-than-life villain of *Mr India*, played by Amrish Puri, we have not had villains who signify such complexity as Maganlal. As Sharmistha Gooptu writes, 'For the larger part, Hindi film villains, even when they became popular largely always played out the good-versus-evil schema of the epics, the simplified aspect of the Ram-Ravana myth. For truly, when a generation of children did not sleep at night, they might be told stories of Gabbar ... in the bad man's own proud words, "*So ja beta ... nahin toh Gabbar Singh aa jayega.*" It was lines such as these which made Gabbar the legend that he did become, spoken words which brought to life a personality which was not our typical Hindi film hero or villain, but complex, and fascinating for being scary or genuinely amusing, and not digested all at once.'

Maganlal is similar. We love to hear him speak Bengali in that unique non-Bengali accent of his, hear him say *refuz* rather than 'refuse' and call Lalmohan-babu Halwamohan-babu with a kind of mock affection. He makes us love him while successfully getting under our skin each time he bullies Lalmohan-babu. Maganlal Meghraj is one of the main reasons why people want to read and watch *Joi Baba Felunath* again and again. He may be bad, but he is never hateful. In fact, he is always electrifying and produces a kind of odd excitement, which makes bad sexy and magnetic. So much so, his personality even threatens to eclipse the real hero, Feluda, on more than one occasion.

Even in the climax of the film when Feluda avenges the treatment meted to Jatayu, Maganlal manages to win over the audience. It is a tussle between two equally matched men and that's why Feluda's victory tastes better. When he forces Maganlal to say, *'Keto taka chai*, Mr Mitter, *keto taka?'* (How much do you want, Mr Mitter, how much?), it is far more than a victory of good over evil. Maganlal's suffering, which is equally dramatic and spectacular, ends up adding to our admiration for the character. Blinking each time Feluda fires a shot from his favourite Colt .32, we see a different side of Maganlal: that he too is scared and vulnerable. A criminal of his calibre begging for mercy while trying hard not to lose his poise has elevated the climax of *Joi Baba Felunath* into a cinematic classic. And when Maganlal falls into Inspector Tewari's lap in the very same way that Lalmohan-babu had done in his house, the wheel of retribution turns a full circle.

In a Bengal that has been dented by multiple chit fund frauds, the figure of Maganlal continues to be more real to the masses than any of the more sophisticated villains in contemporary Bollywood flicks. Sitting on his gaddi, surrounded by a gang of his own strongmen and operating in hawala mode, Maganlal is a very Bengali villain. Maganlal may not be as devious as Moriarty, but he is firmly rooted in the lives of the people of Bengal in a way that the Moriartys of the literary world never can be.

Another villain with his own fan following is Mandar Bose of *Sonar Kella*. With his ability to captivate kids with his magic tricks, and posing as a globetrotter in his worn-out Bata shoes, there is a touch of the romantic about him. But it is his sense of humour that truly marks Bose out in the pantheon of Feluda's adversaries. You may remember asking Dr Hazra for some money to eat, adding in the same breath, 'Only solid'. And when Hazra asks 'And liquid?', Bose quips back: 'Only Horlicks', with a sheepish grin. As is true of so many characters in various Feluda stories, without Mandar Bose, there is no *Sonar Kella*.

The other villains who deserve special mention and some of whom almost outwit Feluda on occasions include Mahadev Chaudhuri, Naresh Pakrashi and Anantalal Batra. Chaudhuri's fascination for watches and his desperation to get hold of the Perigal Repeater in *Gorosthane Sabdhan*, which pits him against Feluda and even sees him abduct Feluda and Topshe, makes him a far more challenging adversary than any ordinary collector or entrepreneur. He is willing to go the extra yard and isn't afraid of taking Feluda on. His self-confidence, which translates into a degree of overconfidence on occasions, makes him all the more charismatic. And Naresh Pakrashi, the quintessential Bengali romantic with a penchant for collecting travelogues and other rare books, does manage to get one up on Feluda in their first meeting. He is excellent when he says during his first meeting with Feluda, '*Amaar bayash teshatti aar amar kukurer bayas tin. Jate* Doberman. *Bairer lok amar ghare beshikkhon thake seta o pochhondo kore na ... kajei ...*' (I am sixty-three and my dog is three. He is a Doberman by breed and he doesn't like outsiders staying in my house for too song. So...) (makes a gesture forcing Feluda to leave). Finally, in Anantalal Batra we have someone extremely shrewd and cunning. Doubling up as two characters, Batra is as much the backbone of *Joto Kando Kathmandute* as Maganlal Meghraj.

In celebrating fifty years of Feluda, what we also celebrate is the immortality of these unique characters of Bengali literature and celluloid.

In fact, *Feluda@50* allows us an opportunity to revisit each of these creations. It is an occasion to celebrate Sidhu Jyatha, a voracious reader and a man with exemplary social commitment. Sidhu Jyatha is perhaps Feluda's Google, a man of exceptional intelligence and knowledge. In an age where digital technology had not consumed lives, Sidhu Jyatha and his old-school ways of maintaining records – books, journals, magazines and clippings – provided Feluda with many an exigent tip. And it was this octogenarian Jyatha, a man Feluda has the greatest respect for, who comes running to his house to inform him about the Sidikpur plane crash in *Kailashe Kelenkari*, and even offers him money to undertake the investigation. He affectionately tests Topshe on occasions, and stakes a claim to having encouraged Feluda to become a private detective.

Celebrating the Feluda oeuvre is also a chance to relive the old-school charms of Kolkata through the eyes of a well-loved character. New Market is where Feluda gets his freshly made chanachur. It is where they first spot 'Nakal Batra', setting up the mystery in *Joto Kando Kathmandute*. North Kolkatans can venture out to the sweet shop next door for mishti and singara, as Lalmohan-babu would do on his way to Rajani Sen Road. It is still a very north Kolkata ritual to start the day with singara and jilipi from one of the many street-side shops, which are slowly being consumed by the bigger eateries and restaurant chains. And tea drinkers can drink a cup of Darjeeling to toast the half-century-old Prodosh C. Mitter.

Finally, Feluda is also a celebration of Bengaliness. Well read, well travelled, the brightest spark around – he is the best of our youthful aspirations and our dreams. Feluda unites the Bengali diaspora in a manner second to none. The essence of him, however, is pan-Indian; the middle-class man who both challenges the normative (in his unusual profession), yet respects the boundaries of social norms (in his respectful ways, his strong moral fibre). There are Feluda fans across the globe, Feluda dialogues are dropped at many a conversation, and Feluda movies are watched as a matter of ritual. It is this world that will come together to celebrate Feluda and his achievements starting December 2015.

Going Backstage with Feluda

Boria Majumdar

Of the many things I like about Feluda, the three standouts are: his sense of morality, honesty and the tremendous similarity with my father. Feluda epitomizes everything that we have come to associate with an Indian middle-class ethos. His sense of honesty is exemplary, evident best in Ghurghutiyar Ghatona *when he returns the precious set of books given to him by the murderer, saying he won't accept books from a criminal. He shares most of his traits with my father – his voracious appetite for books, his love for travel, his social commitment and, finally, his transnational outlook.* – Sandip Ray

Unlike all of us, for Sandip Ray, Feluda has been a very special association. Feluda was created by his father when Sandip was a toddler. In fact, to an extent it was created for him and for many of his generation. He saw Feluda grow up with him, evolve into a cult and gradually assumed responsibility of keeping Feluda alive. 'I would eagerly wait for the Feluda illustrations, which Baba did, read the stories the moment they were published, before Baba started handing them to me for comments when I was slightly older, and when I turned film-maker my first thought was to start with a Feluda film. I did not because I knew there would be unfair comparisons and started with *Fatikchand*. But Feluda was always there for me. He was in a way my responsibility. I had to keep him alive, nurture him, to ensure he continued to be loved by readers and viewers alike. That's what I have tried to do for the last two decades and more,' says Sandip.

There is little doubt Sandip Ray has been instrumental in keeping alive, indeed growing, the cult of Feluda with his numerous celluloid versions of the detective, starting with *Baksha Rahasya* in 1996. So well entrenched is our hero on the screen today that it is with surprise that I listen to Sandip Ray talk about how every Feluda film is inevitably accompanied by chaos.

Mired in Financial Trouble

Feluda, at least in his screen adaptations, has never had it easy. Sandip Ray's efforts to make the films had hit a serious roadblock in the middle of the 1990s. Keen to have the movie ready for the occasion of Prodosh Mitter's thirtieth anniversary in 1995, Sandip Ray had approached every possible producer in Bengal, big and small. Unbelievably, every one of them felt that Feluda doesn't sell. 'Not a single producer came forward. Some even said that Feluda is only for children and by the mid-1990s things had moved on in the industry. Without a proper woman character in the film, and in the absence of sex, love and romance, producers felt it just wouldn't work. I had no option but to drop the idea of making Feluda for the big screen at the time.'

Frustrated at the multiple rebuffs, Ray, who picked Sabyasachi Chakrabarty as Feluda (in a particularly brilliant bit of casting) and Rabi Ghosh as Lalmohan-babu in trying to give a new life to the character, opted to make *Baksha Rahasya* as a telefilm. 'Casting Rabi-da as Lalmohan-babu was a difficult call. Santosh Dutta had made the character immortal and for anyone to play the character was tough. Rabi-da was my best bet, given his versatility as an actor,' says Sandip. However, none of it really helped. No one came forward to put the end product on air because telefilms weren't in vogue at the time, Ray explains. Had he made a teleserial, rather than a telefilm, he would have had more success – at least that is what the industry feedback was. 'I was desperate. The product was ready. Somehow I needed to showcase it to fans, but I wasn't able to. I really did not know what to do for a while,' he says, during one of our many interactions in the course of working on this book. That's when he decided to revive Satyajit Ray Productions, a film distribution company that had not done much work till then. He also contacted Chhayabani, which had distributed many Satyajit Ray films. The owners of Chhayabani assured him that they would put in the money, and release *Baksha Rahasya* as a telefilm in Nandan Two under the auspices of Satyajit Ray Productions.

In the credits the movie is mentioned as jointly produced by Satyajit Ray Productions and Chhayabani, with Chhayabani providing the distribution money. Nandan Two was booked for a month and, in a first in Bengali film industry, a telefilm was released in this way. For four straight weeks, *Baksha Rahasya* played to packed houses at Nandan. Each of the three shows, every single day, was a sell-out. 'It was just incredible to see the thousands of Feluda fans turn up to see *Baksha Rahasya*. There were queues that were a mile long and people were euphoric to see Feluda make a comeback. I spent hours in Nandan trying to soak it all up. It also meant that people had not rejected Benu (Sabyasachi) and Rabi-da. You might want to go and watch Feluda for who he is for the first time, but repeat viewing could only happen if the film had merit. That's what had given me the most satisfaction,' says Ray.

So, did the success of *Baksha Rahasya* enable financing of future films? No, nothing changed at all. The packed halls did nothing to convince producers that a Feluda film would work for the big screen. If anything, their objections grew stronger: what may have worked as a telefilm would never work for the big screen. The two mediums had their own dynamics, profoundly different from each other. Ray's only hope was to keep Feluda alive on the small screen and not give up, like Feluda never does.

In the world of television, however, the success of *Baksha Rahasya* had not gone unnoticed. Within weeks of its release at Nandan, Sandip Ray received a proposal to make a thirty-part Feluda series to commemorate the thirtieth anniversary of the sleuth. The producer was keen to buy the title rights of *Baksha Rahasya* as well, but Ray would have to break it down for television, so it could be serialized. 'With nothing else working, this was the only option to keep Feluda going,' he says. 'I agreed to do the series and set to work.'

He chose his stories carefully, trying to rein in the ever-increasing budget and always conscious of the constraints of working in television. International travel was out of bounds and even a trip to Mumbai was an ordeal. The second story Sandip filmed was *Gosainpur Sargaram*. To his credit, the core unit of *Baksha Rahasya* had been retained for this excellent rendition of a classic Feluda story. Rabi Ghosh, while never as good as Santosh Dutta, was a competent Jatayu. Feluda was clearly working on television.

Interestingly, *Gosainpur Sargaram* was not to be the second Feluda film on air had it all gone to plan. Ray was keen to slot one of the smaller films, like *Sheyal Debota Rahasya*, before he moved on to *Gosainpur*. But destiny had other plans. 'We were doing the last bit of editing for *Gosainpur* and I literally had Rabi-da's face in front of me on the screen when someone came and informed us that he had passed away. All of a sudden, all hell had broken loose. We stopped working in an instant and rushed to Rabi-da's house.'

With Rabi Ghosh no more, Ray telecast *Gosainpur Sargaram* – a very personal tribute to the versatile Rabi Ghosh. *Gosainpur* was a long film and could easily be broken into five parts, allowing Ray over a month to recast Lalmohan-babu. With *Feluda 30* on air, he could no longer abandon the project and walk away. He needed a Lalmohan-babu, and quickly. That's where Anup Kumar came in, and the *Feluda 30* series continued its successful run on the small screen.

By the time *Feluda 30* wound up six months later, telefilms had emerged as the new trend. There was now funding available for telefilms, and it was no surprise that Ray was approached by ETV to make a Feluda film for television. He picked *Dr Munshir Diary* for the project. 'I had reconciled myself to the fact that Feluda had no takers for the big screen. Rather than cribbing and feeling frustrated about the situation, I was better off doing Feluda for television. Something was better than nothing.'

It was the success of *Dr Munshir Diary* that finally changed things for Sandip Ray's Feluda ventures. The old sleuth had takers at the turn of the millennium too. Ramoji Rao, the head of ETV, was looking for a foray into the Bengali film industry and was advised by some of his close associates that Feluda might not be a bad option to start with.

'It is interesting to think that Feluda returned to the big screen at the behest of someone who hardly knew who Prodosh Mitter was. Ramoji Rao had not read any of the Feluda mysteries. Nor had he seen *Sonar Kella* or *Joi Baba Felunath*. In the absence of anyone from Bengal coming forward, it was Rao who gave a new fillip to Feluda by agreeing to fund *Bombaiyer Bombete*. However, things weren't very smooth with him either. When he first saw the film, he was crestfallen. He said as much to me on the phone and had even grieved to his associates that all his money had been wasted on this effort. He was convinced *Bombete* would not run. It was only when the film had run to packed houses for 100 consecutive days that I decided to call him. A delighted Ramoji Rao said to me that his respect for the discerning Bengali film audience had gone up multiple times having seen the way *Bombete* was received.'

The commercial success of *Bombaiyer Bombete* created a new buzz around Feluda. But producers are a hard lot to convince. The Bansals, who had produced *Joi Baba Felunath* in 1979, approached Sandip Ray to do something for them with the precondition that it would have to be something other than Feluda. Sandip agreed. 'We had a long history with them and there was no reason for me to say no. I went ahead on the assumption that if I could make a success of the first film I could very well make Feluda as the second film as part this new association.' The first film, *Nishijapon*, was a reasonable success, and Sandip soon mooted the idea of *Tintorettor Jishu* to the Bansals. Inspired by the success of the first project, they agreed.

But trouble was round the corner. More than halfway into the project, the producers backed off. There was no option but to stop the shoot and take stock. The film needed a producer on board if it was to have any chance of completion, and the new person would first have to deal with the Bansals to clear rights issues and other formalities. 'It was extremely embarrassing, to say the least. Here I was planning to wrap up *Tintorettor Jishu* and planning its release, and all of a sudden, I was told my producer had backed off. It was not the best situation to be in. Multiple media reports added to the negativity and I needed a way out of the mess as soon as possible.'

Such was the uncertainty surrounding *Tintorettor Jishu* that when Mou Roychowdhury and Sumita Sarkar came forward to produce *Kailashe Kelenkari*, Sandip Ray had no option but to shelve the half-done movie and work on the fresh project. 'No one knew what would happen to *Tintorettor Jishu*. I was keen to make Feluda and the best option was to change track and make *Kailashe Kelenkari*. It was the success of *Kailashe Kelenkari* that prompted Mou to come back and negotiate with the Bansals and resurrect *Tintorettor Jishu*,' recalls Ray.

In fact, it was while returning from Aurangabad, where *Kailash* was filmed, that Ray was first asked if he would like to go ahead and finish *Tintoretto*. 'Of course I wanted to. The project had progressed to plan and I would be foolish not to want to finish it. Also, the timing was important. *Kailash* was complete and would be released in a few months. If I wasn't able to get started with *Tintorettor Jishu* soon enough, the project would look dated and the entire effort would be wasted.'

Mou Roychowdhury and her associates approached the Bansals and managed to buy out the rights, prompting a swift restart to the project. 'That's how the project was revived and thereafter there was no problem in finishing the film,' Ray says.

Since then, in a dramatic 180-degree turnaround, everyone wanted a piece of Feluda. Unlike in the 1990s, when Ray had to go from door to door to request funding for a Feluda adventure, producers were lining up at his Bishop Lefroy Road residence, asking him to make the next Feluda. 'Now almost everyone wants a Feluda film. Some of them are keen to sign me up for three films, provided one of them is a Feluda adventure. It is the exact opposite of what the ground reality was in the 1990s. So much so that I am often left wondering where all these people were when I was desperately looking to get some backing to bring Feluda back on the big screen,' Ray says, the agitation evident still. 'It goes to demonstrate the fickle nature of our industry.'

More Trouble for Feluda

The financial strife is only one part of the story. The shooting of every Feluda adventure has had its own trail of chaos. Not a single Feluda film thus far has gone according to plan. The trouble brewing in these backstage stories are on occasion no less thrilling than the adventures themselves.

It all started with the very first Feluda film, the now legendary *Sonar Kella*. A very young Sandip Ray, who had accompanied his father to Rajasthan at the time, remembers that the shoot was methodically planned. In an age when there was no mobile phone or computer, human efficiency served as a more-than-able replacement for these gadgets. The directorial crew had a whole railway bogey to themselves, and as soon as they disembarked in Jodhpur, there was a fleet of cars waiting to take them to the circuit house. 'Rooms had been allocated and every little detail had been planned and implemented meticulously by our production controller, Anil Chaudhuri,' Ray recalls. In Rajasthan in general, and Jaisalmer in particular, the unit made a number of interesting acquaintances in the course of the shoot. One such was a police officer who was posted there at the time. Fortuitously perhaps, the officer used a Colt .32, the revolver Feluda uses in the climax of the film. Satyajit Ray had spoken to the officer and he was more than delighted to provide his revolver to Soumitra Chatterjee to use in the film's climax. But when the crew finally reached Jaisalmer to film the climax, they were told that the officer had been transferred and with him had 'vanished' the much-needed Colt .32! Anil Chaudhuri, not one to give up, made a number of phone calls to his contacts in Jodhpur. He then travelled to Jodhpur overnight to get Ray his much-needed prop for the climax.

Soumitra Chatterjee speaks at some length in his recollections in this book about how the entire climax for *Sonar Kella* was shot inside four hours on the last day of the shoot. The crew had booked the railway bogey for a particular number of days and had to board the return train the following day from Jodhpur, making it imperative for Satyajit Ray to wrap up the Jaisalmer shoot within a specified time frame. A delay meant missing the train from Jaisalmer to Jodhpur that evening, and in turn missing the train from Jodhpur to Delhi. Satyajit Ray heard what his production controller had to say and, to quote Sandip Ray, 'set to work'.

With everything sketched out in his head, Satyajit Ray managed to pull it off, braving the mist and fog. However, the master had missed one thing: he had not filmed Mukul crying. When the realization dawned on the child protagonist that he was finally alone, he just burst into tears, a sequence that adds tremendous potency to the film. 'For this shot, we had to recreate the set in Kolkata, but other than that, Baba had finished everything in the little time we had left. It appears surreal to think that it had indeed been done,' Sandip Ray says.

Joi Baba Felunath, released five years after *Sonar Kella*, also had its share of commotion. The hype around the film was such that, on one particular day, Satyajit Ray had to cancel the shoot because of the huge crowd that had gathered in the Bengali mohalla in Varanasi. People were peeping out of every possible vantage point, windows and verandas even, to see the shoot. Unable to control the crowd, Satyajit Ray was forced to abandon the shoot and return to his hotel. Sensing that he was miffed and could even cancel the shoot as a consequence of what had happened, a group of representatives from the local Bengali community met him in the hotel that evening and promised all cooperation, including crowd management. They requested that he go ahead with the shoot the next morning.

As Sandip Ray says, 'None of us were convinced the promises would be honoured. How could a group of people control or manage a crowd of thousands? More significantly, how could you stop people from peeping out of their windows? The situation was such that Baba was contemplating relocating the shoot to a different location. However, when we went to the location the following morning, we were amazed to see things all calm and quiet. Not a single face was peeping out of a window and no one was standing on any balcony. It was as if there was a curfew in the area. Baba was absolutely delighted with the outcome and went ahead with the shoot without any further hassle after profusely thanking the locals for their help.'

Father to Son: The Chaos Continues

That tradition of chaos remains unbroken, the stories just as good. 'In shooting *Bombaiyer Bombete*, the situation was completely mad,' Sandip ruminates with a smile. Once again, it was the climax that caused the most trouble. Araku in Andhra Pradesh, a stronghold of producer Ramoji Rao, was identified as the site for the final shoot. It was easier to organize a difficult shoot at a place where the producer had contacts and could get things to move if the crew got stuck. Accordingly, Sandip and his 100-plus crew landed in Araku to shoot the train sequence where Victor Perumal, under instructions from Feluda, jumps into the train from his horse to help Feluda expose producer Gopinath Gorey. Sandip Ray was thrilled to see that the train had been arranged and was all set for the shoot to begin. On the morning of the shoot, Ray was told that while they had arranged for the train, they did not have permission that allowed it to move. Unless the train moved, the sequence could not be filmed. Stunned and perplexed, Ray was eventually forced to cancel the shoot and return to Kolkata, incurring significant losses as a result.

After this, it was an ordeal to convince the producer to continue to back the film, and it was a whole month before Ray got a call that he could go ahead with the project. Yet again, all plans were made, and the huge crew once again travelled to Araku to finish off the shoot. This time round, they had a new adversary to contend with: the weather. 'It just rained and rained all night. None of us slept and were constantly looking at the skies and wondering what would happen if the rain did not stop. If the ground was muddy and slushy, it would be impossible to film the crucial final sequence. Finally at day break the rain stopped, and as luck would have it, the sun came out in all its glory, drying out the slushy area in a matter of hours. It seemed the elements were testing us.' This time round, the train moved and Ray managed to wrap up *Bombaiyer Bombete*, which ran for more than a hundred days in cinema theatres across Bengal. It is considered to be one of the most successful Bengali films of recent times.

If the train was at the heart of all the trouble in *Bombete*, it was the airport in *Tintorettor Jishu*. In passing through the X-ray scanner at the airport on the way back from Hong Kong, close to three-fourths of the films reels, which included the entire Hong Kong shoot, was damaged. Sagnik Chatterjee, currently engaged in making a ninety-minute documentary film on Feluda, the release of which is round the corner, remembers the nightmare well. 'We worked 24/7 for three-and-a-half months to digitally restore the full Hong Kong shoot. Most of the reels had base fog and it was a Herculean task to start with. It was painstaking and nerve-wracking at the same time. The entire unit was committed to doing our best and finally we managed to get it all back and finish the film.'

Ray, while showing me the *Tintoretto* portrait which he had commissioned for the film and which now has a pride of place in his house, says much the same. 'It took us all a little time to come to terms with what had happened. Only after we had figured out the problem could we think of a solution. It was extremely difficult, to say the least. More so because we were anticipating a possible problem if the reels were X-rayed more than once and had even requested the security personnel to make an exception. They weren't willing to listen and as a result we had a serious crisis on our hands...' He tails off with his customary smile.

There is no dearth of troublesome climaxes in Feluda movies. The final scenes of *Kailashe Kelenkari*, many will remember, was shot inside Cave 16 at Ellora near Aurangabad. Having planned the whole shoot meticulously, Ray and his team reached Ellora only to be told that Parambrata Chatterjee, playing Topshe, had suddenly contracted measles. Sandip had two options before him: find a new Topshe in forty-eight hours or cancel the shoot. He returned to Kolkata, having cancelled the shoot. 'It is while doing *Kailashe Kelenkari* that I realized the importance of a mobile phone. Had it not been for mobile technology, we would have lost huge monies with Param falling sick. A lot of the equipment was coming to Aurangabad from other cities and we would have ended up paying for it all, had we not cancelled things on time.' Ray laughs and admits that he now uses his wife's mobile on occasion.

That wasn't the end of his woes, though. With Chatterjee back on his feet, Ray went back to his meticulous planning, getting the permissions in place, so they could shoot in a few months. 'Once we reached Kailash, we were all stunned to see that the whole of Cave 16 was under scaffolding. Restoration work was on and despite having all the necessary permissions to shoot, there was little that we could do.'

Not one to give up, Ray began asking around if there was a senior Bengali public servant in the Aurangabad area, someone to whom Feluda would mean something. His search wasn't unsuccessful. Meanwhile, Chakrabarty and Chatterjee had both set off from Aurangabad for Ellora to get started with the shoot.

'We anticipated them midway and asked them to return to Aurangabad to meet this gentleman,' Sandip remembers. The civil servant turned out to be a Sabyasachi fan, and his son a Parambrata fan. Having heard the problem, he told Ray that he'd open the scaffolding part by part, and that the shoot should be planned accordingly. The whole shoot had to be fundamentally reworked, and it was only at the very end that they managed to get the whole cave unhindered and without scaffolding.

Royal Bengal Rahasya brought with it a different set of challenges. Ray shot the movie in three different jungles to recreate the real feel of the story. The scene that proved to be the most difficult was the one with the snake. Ray was absolutely certain that the snake must not be hurt or harmed, and even changed the original storyline to that end. In the film, all he wanted Feluda to do was to carry the cobra – which was coiled up, guarding the Narayani roupyamudra (Narayani silver coins) – out of the temple. Chakrabarty, a wildlife fanatic himself, was happy to do the shot. In Ray's words, 'It could have been one of the high points of the film. Benu brought the cobra out with a smile, and all I wanted him to do was release it, so that I could film it wandering off into the jungle. However, it soon turned out that each time Benu tried to release the cobra, it would just stay put on the same spot for a few minutes before starting to move. That's what snakes generally do is what we were told. The sequence needed the snake to wander away into the jungle for it to have the necessary impact. When we realized that it wasn't going to happen, we did the whole thing digitally.' That *Royal Bengal Rahasya* turned out to be one of the best Feluda films is a tribute to this sort of perseverance and attention to detail.

But the *Badshahi Angti* shoot was to outdo all the others. It all started rather tamely. The bureaucrat who had helped in facilitating the Lucknow shoot requested Ray to allow him to be a part of the project on one of the days. Ray invited him over on the day he was filming at a Café Coffee Day. Within minutes after his arrival, it was apparent that the bureaucrat wasn't happy just watching the shoot. He wanted to be in it. This too wasn't a problem. Ray asked him to sit in the table behind Feluda and Topshe. His only condition was that no one in the frame should look into the camera; they should chat casually in the background. Soon after the shot, the civil servant asked Ray if he could see how it all looked. He was shown the shot in the digital monitor. The man flew into a rage, and asked Ray to retake the shot. 'He started screaming, saying how I could keep him out of focus! It was almost as if he was questioning my ability as director. Not satisfied, he literally ordered me to do a retake with the focus firmly on him. I said to myself that if I had to keep this gentleman in focus, Feluda and Topshe would go out of the frame. Every member of the unit was livid and many came up to me to suggest I should just ask him to leave the sets. Abir was so angry that he could even have hit the fellow for shouting at me. However, having been in the profession for more than three decades now, I have learnt to keep my cool. I knew we still had two weeks of shooting left in Lucknow, and any confrontation could be counterproductive for us in the long run. If the person turned vindictive, he could make life difficult for us in the next few days. It wasn't West Bengal where everyone knows us well and would do things to help us. I hardly knew people in Lucknow, and there was always a risk of running into unexpected roadblocks.'

Ray silently digested the insult and redid the shot, keeping the angry sarkari babu in focus. Yet again, after the shot was done, the man wanted to see the final take. Clearly he had little faith in the director's ability. This time round, the babu was satisfied and finally left, delaying the crew by over two hours. It was money and time wasted, and more importantly, the momentum had been broken. 'I am sure the gentleman must have seen the film and must be thinking we have let him down. To be honest there was little we could do. Had he behaved with a bit of dignity and poise, I would surely have kept him in the shot. But to ask to be the centre of attraction … That would mean a serious disservice to the film itself,' says Ray.

Civil servants are hardly the only ones that wield their petty power with ill grace. In Lucknow, Ray and his team had a run-in with a certain 'law enforcement' machinery as well. They had all the requisite permissions to shoot inside the Bhulbhulaiya in the Bara Imambara. One of Lucknow's central tourist attractions, the Bhulbhulaiya is a central presence in *Badshahi Angti*, because Feluda uses it as a safe place to protect the ring from miscreants.

Ray's unit was in Lucknow just three months before the 2014 parliamentary elections and there was political tension brewing in and around the Imambara at the time. Some political groups, in an attempt to polarize the local electorate, declared that shooting inside the Bhulbhulaiya would be 'haram'. By doing so, Ray would be violating the sanctity of the place. This was a strange declaration given that every tourist visiting the site takes photographs and videos of the place. Ray, failing to reason things out with this bigoted moral police, sought help from the local authorities who had been instrumental in facilitating permissions for the shoot. Alarmingly, they said, 'We will do everything we can to help with the shoot outside the Imambara. Inside, however, it is a different world.'

Ray was annoyed. 'We decided to take one final chance by trying to shoot early in the morning. The Imambara opens at 6 a.m. and the entire unit was there by 5.45, waiting for the gates to open. The plan was to go in and finish things off as quickly as possible. Our local guide and line producers were all there, and all of the unit members were keen to get going with the plan.

However, seeing us assemble outside, the staff looked unhappy. We could sense a brewing unease among a section of them. None of them said anything to us directly, but some of them were seen making calls to friends, trying to apprise them of what was going on. Soon our guide came up to me and said trying to shoot inside would be a serious risk, for the men who had warned us the day before wouldn't hesitate to cause us bodily harm. There was a risk that the equipment could be targeted. Local youth from around the area had been summoned and it wasn't working out well. We were there to shoot Feluda and not a political documentary. It wasn't worth the effort, and I was unwilling to put the entire unit at risk. There is no question I was disappointed. Everyone was. We decided to cancel the shoot and I asked Shirsha to come back at a later time and take a few shots of the place. With what is available on the web, and with what Shirsha managed to get, we created the set in Kolkata on our return and filmed the sequence. Also, in the book, Feluda and Topshe meet Mahavir Seth inside the Imambara. I had wanted to film this sequence on the terrace of the Imambara looking out over Lucknow. It offered a spectacular view, and would have added much to the film. However, it wasn't to be, and eventually the meeting took place just outside the Imambara on the street where Mahavir is seen getting off his car. It wasn't the best for the film but there was little else we could do,' Ray says matter-of-factly.

If the Imambara was a disappointment, the travel from Haridwar to Lakshman Jhoola was an eye opener. In Satyajit Ray's original, the area is described as a hilly terrain with dense jungles, which is exactly as it was close to half a century earlier. Since then, however, things have changed – and how! Trying to find a location to film the climax, Sandip Ray and his team drove from Haridwar to Lakshman Jhoola. Today, there are no jungles there. Clusters of houses have come up across this entire stretch.

'I asked the driver if this was the only route from Haridwar to Lakshman Jhoola and was told that this was the shortest route. There was another more roundabout route. I wanted to explore if that was any better. It wasn't. While there were some spots of uninhabited land, there was nothing in the area where I could film the climax. Yet again, the only option was to film the scene somewhere else. That's why I chose Jhargram. I knew I could control things in West Bengal better, and Jhargram offered us a very similar location to what Baba has described in *Badshahi Angti*. The wooden house would look apt if recreated in the middle of the tall trees. And the roads too were decent enough to go ahead with the plan. While this added to the expense and to the time taken to complete the project, it did get the film closer to the original story, which is so very essential in a Feluda film. The feedback I got about the location of the climax was good and that's what matters in the end.'

But the Story Moves On

At the end of all of these stories, the only question I ask Sandip Ray is, 'Is it still worth the effort?' Does he ever feel demotivated because of these trials and tribulations?

'Let me be totally honest with you. I had never imagined Feluda would become the cult that he has. I can assure you Baba would have agreed with me. From *Feludar Goendagiri* to today, it has been an incredible journey. With each novel, the cult has grown and now with each film, the demand is for more. As a film director, I am also an entertainer. And in trying to entertain millions of Feluda fans, I am willing to undertake any level of stress. When I see fans queue up to watch Feluda and thereafter see them come out smiling, it seems to me that every effort is worth it. Each of my unit members, who are more family than anything else, feels the same. And while you may ask how I could possibly keep my composure in these situations, you must remember I am never alone. First, I have learnt it from Baba. And now there are close to eighty of us together at any given point. That's a huge strength. We face every situation as a team. We travel and dine together, discuss plans and seek out solutions. That's the challenge that every project brings in its wake and that's how things are and always will be. Finally, we have Feluda with us. He will inevitably find a way, however tight a spot he may be in. Using his magajastro, he will come up trumps in the end. It has been the case since 1973 when *Sonar Kella* was filmed. Good things always happen to good people.'

Part Two

Felu Mittir: Between Bhadrolok and Chhotolok

Indrajit Hazra

In the summer of 1965, a character who would go on to become a cult classic for Bengali youngsters – and subsequently for Bengali adults nostalgic for both their formative years as well as for the 1960s–80s – was born.

He was a barrel-chested youngster with a boyish face, always seen in a pair of proto-lycra black shorts ('half-pant') and sleeveless orange vest ('genji'). He was the affable neighbourhood dada who, instead of being the local bully, got things sorted out, especially when it came to the two deviously wicked kids who were forever his adversaries. In fact, this strongman youngster with his ninety-six-inch chest was what the archetypal Bengali young man was not: muscular and 'un-intellectual'.

Illustrator Narayan Debnath created this cartoon character, Bantul 'the Great', as a visual slapstick comic strip aimed at the readers of the children's magazine, *Shuktara*. Unlike its more illustrious and literary counterpart, *Sandesh*, *Shuktara* was racy – and more popular. I recall gorging on the weekly through the 1970s and '80s, with Bantul on the cover announcing my life's weekly cycle.

Bantul arrived quietly, and suddenly burst on the scene only a few months later during the 1965 India–Pakistan war when Narayan depicted him whirling Pakistani tanks by their nozzles Incredible Hulk–style. The *Shuktara*'s young readers wouldn't have realized it then, but this Bengali neighbourhood strongman was really a literal, cartoon riposte to Lord Macaulay's withering description of (Hindu upper and middle class) Bengali men having a 'feeble constitution' and being 'effete, effeminate, vaporous, swooning'.

That Bantul of the comic is, at best, simple and, at worst, downright stupid is obvious from Debnath's simple narrative and unsophisticated lines. Tom and Jerry appeal to kids until a certain age – after which they become fodder for the nostalgia machine.

Which is perhaps why it was left to another character to simultaneously be a counter and a counterpart to this anomalous no-brain and all-brawn Bengali pop icon. Only a few months after Bantul was single-handedly pulverizing Pakistani tanks, there appeared on the pages of *Sandesh*, a sharp young man not averse to action – Prodosh C. Mitter, or Felu, or as his cousin-cum-sidekick would immortalize him: Feluda.

Satyajit Ray is today more popular among Bengalis for his Feluda stories – and cinematic adaptations of two of them – than his films. During his lifetime, Ray certainly earned far more from his books than his movies, and his Feluda catalogue remains a best-seller to this day. The franchise continues to release one adventure after another every year before Durga Pujo or Christmas, courtesy Ray's film-maker son, Sandip.

But even before December 1965, when the first instalment of *Feludar Goendagiri* was published in *Sandesh*, the character was already formed in Ray's head, not necessarily as the twenty-seven-year-old strictly amateur detective, but as a repository of cosmopolitan sharpness who was healthily sceptical of Bengali middle-class behaviour and thinking, while at the same time being in the thick of that middle-classness.

Feluda's origins can be found in the run-up to his delivery into the world in the winter of 1965. In May 1965, Ray released the dual-story film *Kapurush-o-Mahapurush* (The Coward and the Holy Man). The first film, based on the writer and poet Premendra Mitra's short story 'Jonoiko Kapurusher Kahini' (A Certain Coward's Story), highlighted a particular kind of cowardice that afflicted the middle-class protagonist – one that Ray is happy to skewer.

Mitra's story starts with a woman bringing the narrator a cup of tea. Within a few paragraphs, the reader recognizes two things: it is a middle-class Bengali setting, with the two characters maintaining an enforced air of politeness. We quickly realize that the two were once lovers. Some years before, Koruna, the woman, had urged him that they elope before her family packs her off to Patna. He had made comforting noises but then did nothing. This time, things are much more ambiguous, as the protagonist asks Koruna to leave her husband – who provides him with an overnight stay while his car is being repaired in the garage – and go away with him.

Whether he does so flippantly, neither the reader nor Koruna knows – until the end when Koruna does appear at the station platform. Again, he takes no action. But this time round, the woman tells the protagonist (and us) that she was actually joking and that she had actually come to the station to retrieve the sleeping pills she had given him the night before. Mitra ends the story with the page crackling with dissimulation and disappointment, and a strange aftertaste of something almost comic.

In the film adaptation, Ray makes this tragi-comic tone the pivot of the story. He starts linearly enough, with the actor Soumitra Chatterjee as the protagonist, a screenwriter travelling around in his car in north Bengal to 'research' his next screenplay. But Ray heightens certain features to highlight his ultimate cowardice. When offered a whisky by his host, Koruna's tea-estate husband, he declines and nurses his sherry suspiciously through the evening as the other man gets progressively intoxicated in a tea-estate burra saheb way. Ray is keen to underline the hero's effeteness, as he shows him pleading with his old flame, when they are alone, to come away with him.

It is worthwhile to know Ray's own antipathy towards 'naekami', that untranslatable Bengali word that suggests affectation and pretension laced with syrupy melodrama. He recalled his unwillingness to join Visva-Bharati in Santiniketan as a student because he had heard the boys there were naeka. The Coward in *Kapurush* is infused with this dreaded and dreadful naekami.

Is it too much of a leap to believe that a few months after making *Kapurush*, Ray would invent a detective character that was Un-Kapurush, not only in the sense of being fearless, but also in terms of being unblemished by that singularly Bengali virus of naekami? Thus, Feluda's fetish for reason, deduction, facts and sarcasm. Arguably, he is one of the least talkative mystery solvers in the genre, his trusted and in-awe sidekick Topshe noticing long bouts of silence.

But if *Kapurush* set up a template of what Feluda would *not* be, indeed be the opposite of – and an apples-to-apples comparison could be easily made once Soumitra Chatterjee makes his first appearance as Feluda in *Sonar Kella*, nine years after his role in *Kapurush-o-Mahapurush* perhaps injects a chief ingredient of what would be the warp and woof of Feluda stories: uncovering mysteries and exposing villains.

Mahapurush is based on the 1929 satirical short story 'Birinchi Baba' by Rajshekhar Bose, under his nom de guerre Parashuram, where a god-man descends on a neighbourhood and has everyone eating off his palm. (Bose's brother, incidentally, was the family doctor in the Ray household and a friend of Sigmund Freud.)

Ray sticks to the structure of Bose's story. But he puts his own indelible stamp – and of his notion of the typical middle- and upper-class psyche of contemporary Kolkata which goes beyond 'the Bengali' – in that he comes down less strongly on the god-man, the Mahapurush, than on the people ready and willing to be duped by him.

In fact, one of the characters raring to expose the charlatan admits in the film, 'The man is talented. He's a top-class actor, understands mass psychology, is knowledgeable, has an amazing memory, has imagination, has presence of mind and has guts. What else does one need?' How much of Birinchi Baba did Ray still retain in the character of Machhli Baba in the Feluda story *Joi Baba Felunath*? Certainly, Varanasi's smuggler-charlatan Machhli Baba is far more vicious and less fascinating than Bose–Ray's god-man. But what's material here is the trope of exposing what is hidden or fake through the genre of a detective series – which in a way is what Mahapurush/Birinchi Baba is if one takes away the whiplash of social satire.

Whether it's the fake Dr Hazra (as opposed to the real Dr Hajra) in the 1971 Feluda novel, *Sonar Kella* or the fake Rudrashekhar in the 1982 novel *Tintorettor Jishu*, or even fake objects, such as the bejewelled Ganesha idol in *Joi Baba Felunath*, imposters abound in Feluda's universe.

The fake, the imposter, the charlatan hold a special appeal for the detective/mystery genre writers and their heroes. Ray and Feluda are no exception. But the special appeal for exposing them through stories and a hero that mirrors Ray's own ambivalent relationship with the Bengali middle-class psyche needs a proper Feluda-esque investigation.

Feluda is my maternal cousin.[1] I am fourteen, and he is twenty-seven. Some call him half-insane, some eccentric, and some others call him lazy. But I know that at his age, there are few as intelligent as Feluda. And if he gets a job that's worth his while, there are very few people who can work as hard as he does. Apart from that, he plays good cricket, knows almost a hundred-odd indoor games, knows card tricks, knows a little hypnotism, and can write with both his left and right hands. And when he used to go to school, his memory was so good that by reading 'Debotar Gras' [a poem by Rabindranath Tagore] twice he could memorize it.

Topshe's description of his cousin in *Badshahi Angti* is that of no-holds-barred hero worship. For a teenage boy in mid-1960s Kolkata, having a brother who tells him how the word 'horrendous' is not a real word but an English neologism that mixes 'horrible' with 'tremendous' is impressive enough. But to have him actually crack cases that older adults, which quickly include police officers, start seeking him out for was exceptional for both the teenage narrator as well as his mostly teenage readers.

When Feluda makes his appearance in 1965–66, he is twenty-seven, making his year of birth 1939. Topshe, on the other hand, is a post-Independence boy. When Feluda was Topshe's age, in circa 1953, Byomkesh Bakshi was already an established detective hero in Bengali households and had just cracked his latest case, documented by his creator Sharadindu Bandyopadhyay in *Chiriakhana* (The Zoo), which Ray would adapt to film in 1967, making his first foray into the detective genre as a film-maker.

---

1 Topshe was Basu, but Ray then changed his name to Mitra. I'm told Feluda explains it like this: Tapesh started out writing the stories as fiction and therefore said that they are maternal cousins, but they are in fact fraternal cousins.

In 1948–49, when Felu Mittir (transliterated into anglicized Bengali as 'Mitter') was ten, and Bandyopadhyay had 'retired' Byomkesh by marrying him off (he would revive him sixteen years later on 'popular demand'), the twenty-eight-year-old Ray had two life-changing events: one, when he met Jean Renoir who was visiting Kolkata in search of locations and actors for his film *The River*; and two, when he got married. Bijoya Ray née Das and Ray were, like Topshe and Feluda, maternal cousins. It is no coincidence that Feluda was let out into the world at large by Ray when the young deducer of facts had reached the age when Manik-da, too found his firm footing in the world.

Kolkata in 1965 was in social and political churn – yet to explode as it would when the Naxalite movement finally came down from the hills of north Bengal in the late 1960s and early 1970s. Facing food shortage in the state, West Bengal chief minister Prafulla Chandra Sen had, a year before, introduced foodgrain rationing and imposed a heavy tax on rice mills. In one stroke, he had invoked the ire of Congress-supporting mill owners as well as the communists, who in 1964 had split, with the breakaway CPI(M) forming the more left contingent than the rump CPI. Economist and former CPI(M) finance minister Ashok Mitra describes those days in his 2003 memoirs *Apila-Chapila* (translated in English as 'A Prattler's Tale' by Sipra Bhattacharya):

> ... a major section of the Bengali middle class was, going by external evidence, itching for a social revolution. Developments in the international political situation were equally of considerable import. The Americans were still angry with India, and we were getting arms and economic aid mostly from the socialist countries. ... In Calcutta the reins seemed to be completely in the grip of the CPI(M). The state government had almost ceased to function. There were strikes, and more strikes, every week: in support of the demand of food, of higher wages, or for the reopening of

closed factories. The strikes literally shut down Calcutta. Never before this had the great city taken on such an appearance of total stillness, and never was the phenomenon to be repeated.

Little wonder that Ray chose the peace of Darjeeling for a 'criminal' rupture to be made in Feluda's first adventure. The first line of the first story, 'I see Rajen-babu come to the Mall every afternoon', conjured up crisp walks and grand views far removed from the storm and stress of a Kolkata under siege and in turmoil. To have situated a mystery in the cauldron of contemporary Kolkata would have drowned out the chaos of the mysterious threatening letters that arrive.

But Feluda's adventures, by themselves, were escape routes by which Ray could stay firmly out of the turmoil and chaos that he found himself surrounded by – not only in his real life in Kolkata but also in his 'serious' movies. Writing children's stories with a detective hero and set in exotic locations, perforce, kept the swirling, disturbances of the world at bay.

Even in the novel, *Gorosthane Sabdhan*, set in Kolkata and written in four days in 1977, a month after the Left Front government headed by Jyoti Basu surged into power and stayed there for the next thirty-four years, Ray has Feluda say, 'But just think of it, Topshe – an Englishman sitting beside the Ganga, on the edge of a huge wasteland inhabited only by mosquitoes, snakes and frogs, thinks that he will set up business here. And lo and behold, the wilderness is cleared, houses are built, roads are laid out and lighted by rows of gas lights; horses and palanquins start travelling and before a hundred years pass, there grows a city in that place that came to be known as the City of Palaces. *The present disgraceful conditions of the city is not the point.* I am talking about history' (italics added).

Even in his trademark transmission of historical and

geographical facts in all Feluda stories, Ray can't help but let out a snort of disgust. It seems like for a brief moment, in that single sentence, Ray had looked out of the window of his airy study at 1/1 Bishop Lefroy Road, and allowed himself to be contaminated by the 'adult' upheavals underway outside.

In this, Ray was more aware of Feluda's young adult readership that allowed him the luxury of maintaining a clinical, even an antiseptic, distance from contemporary happenings – something that even his favourite sociopathic sleuth Sherlock Holmes wouldn't be allowed by Arthur Conan Doyle in anarchist-ridden, cocaine-peddling, industrial revolutionary Victorian London. Little wonder that, compared to Feluda, Byomkesh seemed dated to the 1960s–80s reader; he was far more anchored to 1940s–50s Kolkata.

Herge's Tintin, another fictional crime-buster Ray greatly admired, and who is closer to Feluda (and Topshe closer to Snowy) than generally recognized, was more in sync with the real world of Chicago mobsters (*Tintin in America*), Latin American dictators (*Tintin and the Picaros*) and post-colonial and pre–World War II oil supplies (*Land of Black Gold*). But it is this atemporality that also allows Feluda mysteries to remain far more 'contemporary' – as evidenced by its continued popularity – than the more noir and violent crime stories of Byomkesh Bakshi for older readers.

But Ray's antipathy towards having Feluda drawn into contemporary political and social settings has a deeper root: he didn't like what he saw happening around him. This bhadrolok abhorred the breakdown of reason, the flood of chaos, unthinking violence and unintelligent criminal acts – even if he had separate problems with middle-class hypocrisy and behaviour. But there was an ambiguity, as is evident in Ray's Calcutta Trilogy – the films *Pratidwandi* (The Adversary, 1970), *Seemabaddha* (Company Limited, 1971) and *Jana Aranya* (The Middleman, 1975) – and in his late film, *Ganashatru* (Enemy of the People, 1989), where Ray does let the political and social muck in.

At the time of writing *Gangtoke Gondogol* and *Sonar Kella* in 1970–71, he wrote to his biographer and friend Marie Seton describing Calcutta as a 'nightmare city' and toying with the idea of leaving it. There was a compelling reason why Ray found the chaos outside the world of films and books distasteful: it was personal.

As he told Andrew Robinson (in *Satyajit Ray: The Inner Eye*), 'I might have understood more the young peoples' minds if my son had taken to that movement. But he was a victim. Sandip was surrounded and threatened with a dagger when he turned up for his BA exams. They told him, "You are the son of Satyajit Ray. We'll see how you can pass this examination."' But there was another reason for Ray's desire to remain an 'apolitical' film-maker and writer. He found getting artistically involved unaesthetic.

Which brings us to the nub of the matter: Feluda was the crystallization of Ray's unease with Bengali middle-class straitjacketing and delusional self-imaging, as well as with his natural distaste for the populist, the garish, that somewhere in his mind, slid down to the all-too-visible lumpen. Felu Mittir holds the key to maintaining an equal distance from the ossified bhadrolok (cultured man) and the rampaging chhotolok (lumpen).

Ray's bilingual genius applies not only to his mastery over the languages of Bengali and English, or over his equally vast and deep knowledge in matters Indian and 'Western', but also to his ease with Bengali high and popular culture. Consistently, in his Feluda books, Ray simultaneously tapped and displayed his closeness and fondness for the demotic, his natural affinity towards middle-class colloquialisms.

The early, younger Feluda is particularly comfortable playing the foil, rather than adversary, to Debnath's Bantul the Great or other pop-cultural icons in the Bengali universe. We hear him snap playfully at Topshe with a '*Pakami korishne*' (Don't act smart). He is equally at ease displaying his irritation with lazy reasoning as he is with bad taste. Such as when we meet him in the opening pages of *Gorosthane Sabdhan*, berating Lalmohan 'Jatayu' Ganguly for the second-hand Mark 2 Ambassador he has bought.

> 'Until you change that grotesque horn of yours and get a civilized one instead, that car is forbidden to enter Rajani Sen Road [where Feluda and Topshe live with Topshe's parents].'
>
> Jatayu looked apologetic.
>
> 'I knew I was taking a big risk,' he said, 'but you know the salesman was demonstrating – somehow I couldn't resist the temptation. It's Japanese, you know.'
>
> 'It's ear-splitting and nerve-wracking,' said Feluda. 'I could never have believed that Hindi films would influence you so soon. And that colour – equally unbearable. Just like what you see in Madras films.'

In the 1979 novel, *Chhinnamastar Abhishap*, a quieter, more ironic Felu again takes on Lalmohan, the title of whose new thriller, *Vancouverer Vampire* – in keeping with his proto–Karan Johar alliterative titles – he finds deeply problematic.

Topshe narrates, 'He had said that Vancouver is a very modern city, and for vampires to stay there is impossible. To which Lalmohan-babu replied that after he had scoured through Horniman's geography book, he figured that would be the best title.'

These make for comic situations before the actual adventure begins, or in between situations that call for seriousness. But at some fundamental level, Jatayu is the representative of the Bengali middle-class middle-aged man whom Ray wants to befriend and educate at the same time through Feluda. It would not be an exaggeration to say that Feluda's raison d'être is as much to try and inculcate the likes of Lalmohan Ganguly with the right kind of reasoning (and, by some miracle, the right kind of taste) as it is to solve mysteries.

Which brings us back to the binary Bengali universe of the bhadrolok and chhotolok. The figure of the bhadrolok is quite well established even outside the immediate domain of Bengali cultural politics.

In terms of class, the bhadralok (the female equivalent is bhadromohila, but doesn't quite transfer the same qualities) can range from the archetypal rich, upper-middle-class Bengali gentleman to the middle-class Bengali gentleman whose relative lack of wealth is compensated for by his ability to stand out with dignity in a crowd. Amartya Sen is a bhadrolok. Jyoti Basu, Buddhadeb Bhattacharjee and much of the old guard of the Bengali Left leadership are considered bhadrolok. Lalmohan Ganguly, by dint of his affable nature and jolly spirit, just about makes it into the fold. Satyajit Ray himself was a bhadrolok, however critical of his own tribe he may have been.

The chhotolok (literally 'small man') is a more tricky archetype to bottle. At its most basic, the chhotolok is crass, uncultured, a specimen to be equally feared and be repelled by. Usually he shows signs of drunkenness and lewd behaviour, uses foul language and is terribly devoid of capital C-ed Culture. He would be the one who, if getting his hands on some money, will go out and buy a garish green car with a loud horn. And above everything, he is loud – and is sated by what Feluda disparagingly calls 'Hindi films'.

In the world of criminals and imposters that both Feluda's stories and the world we live in share, the chhotolok has sinister, antisocial overtones. In Feluda's moral universe, he is the vicious villain. Take the two villainous kidnappers in *Sonar Kella*: Bhabananda aka Amiyanath Barman, alias the Great Barman – Wizard of the East, who pretends to be the parapsychologist

Dr Hemanga Hajra, and his partner in crime Mandar Bose. While Barman, the leader of the duo, comes across as the criminal mastermind that he is – 'This man seemed too shrewd. Besides, he was much too tall and formidable-looking. Not at all what we think of when we say, "Dr"' – Mandar Bose is a cut-throat and fits the bill. The talentless ruffian is Ray's chhotolok.

The most obvious 'chhotolok' in the Feluda pantheon of villains, however, is Maganlal Meghraj. Ray via Topshe describes him: 'The eyes that regarded us solemnly were sunk in, set under thick, bushy eyebrows. A blunt nose, thick lips and a pointed chin completed the picture. He too was wearing a kurta-pyjama. The buttons on his kurta might well have been diamonds. Besides these, on eight of his ten fingers flashed other stones of every possible colour.'

Ray's disdain for flashiness – what in present parlance would be 'bling' – immediately sets the oily Maganlal up as a chhotolok villain. To drive the point further home, Ray has the Benarasi Sethji throw Feluda a wad of currency notes as a bribe to stop meddling in the case. 'There is three thousand here, Mr Mittir. Take it. Take it and relax, enjoy yourself with your cousin and uncle.'

In *Satyajit Ray: Portrait of a Director*, Marie Seton points to Ray's very Bengali middle-class bhadrolok attitude towards money. 'Wealth, which once was little respected in comparison to wisdom, now wields more power over the imagination than it ever did before in India. Satyajit, who counted the pennies throughout his youth, seems to have equated wealth with impecuniosity of spirit, if not active evil, in all his films.' The same holds in Ray's depiction of villains in Feluda stories, where the prime motive for villainy is almost always to possess unlawfully what is not that person's property or object of value.

In a note to a Feluda collection, Ray had written in 1988, 'To write a whodunit while keeping in mind a young readership is not an easy task, because the stories have to be kept "clean". No illicit love, no crime of passion, and only a modicum of violence. I hope adult readers will bear this in mind when reading these stories.' Reading this in conjunction with the knowledge that Ray refused to visit brothels for background research in his 1970 film *Pratidwandi*, it seems that Ray found writing 'clean' detective stories for kids a relief. It was also where the usual traits of the chhotolok that he couldn't bear could be conflated in the vice of greed and terrible taste. And it was Feluda who would strike the right balance between the bhadrolok in his bubble and the chhotolok in his den.

Bengali popular literature for young adults has the trinity of 'da-s': Ghanada, Tenida and Feluda.

Ghanashyam Das aka Ghanada is the eldest of the lot, appearing first in the short story 'Mosha' (Mosquito) in 1945. His creator was Premendra Mitra, who had written the comic, supremely satiric short story on which Ray had based his aforementioned film on a god-man, 'Mahapurush'. Ghanada is a teller of tall tales, which he narrates to his all-male younger fellow residents of a mess house. Mitra's hero is a flamboyant bachelor, a sharper, more wicked version perhaps of Feluda's friend Lalmohan Ganguly. His acerbic comments, coupled with his fantastical shaggy dog tales – where he saves the world using a nail, or goes to Mars, or saves the world from a gigantic tidal wave, or points out in a matter-of-fact way that Robinson Crusoe was actually a young woman – make him the mad Socrates of Bengali literature.

Feluda, with his addiction to reason and truth seeking, would have obsessively picked holes in Ghanada's stories, not realizing that the modern mythologist would not have cared. The fact that there is some sort of revival in Ghanada's cult status of late points to the sheer power of the man's ability to conjure up time- and space-neutral fabrications.

Bhojohari Mukhopadhyay aka Tenida is the least known among

the three 'da-s', and not only in the non-Bengali-reading world
any more. This rather nutty character first appeared in Narayan
Gangopdhyay's children's novel *Chaar Murti* (Four Characters) in
1957 as a serialization. Tenida, like Ghanada, is also surrounded
by three hench-boys, and acts out his particular form of hyper-
absurdity. Among the 'da-s', Gangopadhyay's Groucho Marx–like
character is the youngest, although his years of trying to graduate
from school doesn't confirm this possibility.

If Feluda is the atypically rational young Bengali man ready to
go off anywhere to solve a mystery, and if Ghanada is the atypically
imaginative older Bengali man ready to go nowhere but only talk
about 'past journeys criss-crossing the world and beyond', Teni is
the typical Bengali youngster, exaggerated only that much. His lust
for any kind of food and his signature exclamation, 'De la Grande
Mephistopheles' – which is then completed with equal aplomb by
his three sidekicks with 'Yuk!' – place him in the neighbourhood
of all-brawns Bantul. Except that Tenida's maniacal behaviour is
genuinely cartoon-funny.

His world and Feluda's will never cross. And while both Feluda
and Ghanada manage to leave a ticker tape of genuine, exciting
facts about the real world behind after readers have read about
their adventures, Tenida is the odd one out, in that his loud,
neighbourhood-based world is practically extinct.

Satyajit Ray was surely aware of these two cult figures in Bengali
popular literature, especially Ghanada, about whom he must
have read before he turned to the likes of Conan Doyle and those
mysteries for grown-ups by English and American writers. That,
unlike Sharadindu Bandyopadhyay's Byomkesh Bakshi, Ray's
Prodosh Mitter would become a 'da' was a smart move by Ray
aka Manik-da. Topshe would have had to be invented if he didn't
exist – if for nothing else but to be the only person who actually
calls Felu 'Feluda'. We should know; all of us are Topshes.

Feluda's final adventure, *Robertsoner Ruby*, took place in 1991, which helps new readers avoid seeing Ray's hero through sepia tones. Also immensely helpful is the steady supply of the annual cinematic adaptations of Feluda stories, whose thirty-five adventures are ever updatable and ever relatable.

Even as we notice the evolution of Feluda down the years from 1965 to 1991 – made most palpable in Ray's own illustrations – as a proto-man who is a bit more fun-loving and boyish than the hard-chinned man he would grow into being, the most popular character that Ray ever created has been retrofitted to go well with the times. Not because of some reboot or reappraisal of the quite incongruous traits of an intelligent Bengali who is also a man of action. But because Felu Mittir has changed our perception of the Bengali bhadrolok.

Would it be so far-fetched to believe that there is a bit of Feluda in, say, Sourav Ganguly? Or in all those who shared that 'seditious' Facebook post by Ambikesh Mahapatra, the Jadavpur University chemistry professor, depicting West Bengal chief minister Mamata Banerjee and fellow Trinamool leader Mukul Roy with those immortal lines: '*Dekhte pachchho,* Mukul? *Sonar kella*' (Can you see, Mukul, the Golden Fortress), followed by an image of then Union railways minister and out-of-favour TMC leader Dinesh Trivedi with the speech baloon, '*Dushtu lok,* vanish!' (Wicked man vanished!). Or that Lalmohan Ganguly's pitch-perfect comic phrases and moments have become memes of their own.

In a 1996 'Feluda 30' special issue of the *Sandesh* magazine, where Felu Mittir's exploits first appeared in a serialized form, Ray's son had written about how his father, after taking over as the editor of the revived *Sandesh* in 1961, would keep hardcover exercise books in which he scribbled notes. From 1961 to 1964, there was not a word or scratch about any Feluda. Then suddenly, in 1965, in the exercise book's third page, he started *Feludar Goendagiri.*

On the first page, there's just father's signature and year in English. Before a new character is created, normally a writer makes some introductory notes. He hadn't done any of that. Like the other stories he had written over the last four years, he had simply started [with Feluda] right there and then.'

It would be quite romantic to believe that the spirit of Felu Mittir had descended on Manik-da one day in very late 1965. But as Feluda would have said with perfect reason and logic, 'Apply your head, Topshe! Think. That doesn't make any sense. That doesn't make any sense at all.'

* * *

Indrajit Hazra is the author of the novels *The Burnt Forehead of Max Saul, The Garden of Earthly Delights* and *The Bioscope Man*. His non-fiction includes *Grand Delusions: A Short Biography of Kolkata*. He works as a journalist and lives in New Delhi.

Modus Operandi: Two or Three Things I ~~Know~~ About Feluda

Sovan Tarafder

1.

'See how the card has come up!'

Feluda flashed a visiting card off his moneybag and asked me to have a look. Just a few words: Prodosh C. Mitter, Private Investigator. The message, however, is clear. Now he wants to flaunt his investigating acumen…

As early as in the third of his long chain of Feluda stories and novels – *Kailash Choudhuryr Pathor* – Satyajit Ray suggests that the young protagonist of the story, so far moonlighting as a detective, has decided to take the plunge. The story begins with this particular piece of information.

The card-flashing investigator, like Bengali gentry more generally, doesn't mind being called – or even publicly known – by his nickname 'Felu'. It is suffixed with the Bengali honorific 'da', used to denote a person who is considered an elder brother, either by virtue of familial relation or just non-familial reverence.[1]

Although it is not clear what the job might be, in the first two stories, Feluda is described as holding a salaried job, like so many Bengalis of his background. However, in the third one, he appears to have taken up the job of a private investigator as his profession.[2] In the first two stories, Feluda was in Darjeeling and Lucknow (to solve the mysteries, eventually) only because he was on leave. There is no mention of a job in the third story, *Kaliash Choudhuryr Pathor*. So there is the double bind of a certain objective *presence* (visiting card) and an informational *absence* (that he'd been on leave from his service) to confirm the theory. However, neither

---

1 cf. Haroon-da, the central protagonist in Ray's story 'Phatikchand', perfectly embodies the non-familial figure of an elder brother. It seems rather natural that, given the humanist stance that he maintained all along, Ray would not restrict himself to the familial category only while portraying the idea of brotherhood. And, it needs to be noted that the other two famous characters in Bengali literature carrying the suffix 'da' attached to their nickname (a la Feluda) – namely, Ghanada and Tenida – are duly respected and obeyed (like an elder brother is) in the stories by people who do not share any familial relation with them.

2 There is a bit of confusion, though. In the fifth story of the series, *Gangtoke Gondogol*, Feluda is again mentioned to be a service holder. However, it appears to be one of the few irregularities in the Feluda series. After this, Feluda appears as a professional private eye, and is further established as such in the two Satyajit Ray Feluda movies – *Sonar Kella* and *Joi Baba Felunath*. In the latter, Feluda, in his trademark polite yet curt manner, tells the on-duty police inspector that, without any permanent service at hand, a private investigator has to find cases to sustain him.

in this story nor in the entire Feluda corpus is there concrete confirmation of his resignation from that job.

Nevertheless, the fact remains that this particular story onwards, there are direct or oblique references to his stature as a professional private detective.

2.

The third Feluda story was written and published in 1967. In hindsight, it is a fairly unusual year for a Bengali youth (that too based in Calcutta then) to leave an (apparently) permanent job only to pursue the uncertain career of a private investigator. It is, after all, the year that marks the formal beginning of a tumultuous phase in the history of West Bengal. Before we explore that, here's a proposition.

The extraordinary case of Mr Pradosh C. Mitter has, among other things, a significant non-presence of the *real*. This is not meant to undermine either the sleuth's formidable powers of observation, or the author-director's legendary eye for detail. On the contrary, these qualities construct the *reality* of these stories.

Still, this determination to keep Feluda cocooned from the contemporary realities of the time is intriguing in the sense that it is both diegetic and non-diegetic. The sleuth and his sidekick live in Calcutta, and some of the action plays out there. The Calcutta (as the city was called then) of the stories – described in meticulous detail – was not the dystopic city space that people of the time actually lived in. With the complex network of roads, lanes and by-lanes consistent and accurate, the urban topography has never been misrepresented.

Feluda has a deep veneration for history. The *past* is a space Ray does not tamper with. For him, as also for the sleuth he has created, history is the repository of truths that people do not adequately regard. Feluda, in one case after another, finds ways to negotiate with the past. Be it digging the physical space of a grave (*Gorosthane Sabdhan*) or the non-physical space of a riddle that contains a piece of semantic history (*Ghurghutiyar Ghatona*) or a boy who remembers his earlier incarnation (*Sonar Kella*), all of these stories maintain an interesting engagement with the past.

The problem lies with the *present*. Rather with the representation of the *present*. Given the socio-politico-economic setting of the protagonists' circumstances and times, those who people the story are quite plausibly fashioned. The class divide of the Bengali societal structure is perfectly in place. Both the detective and his clients, across rural and urban longitudes, bank on the unorganized labour force (the servant) to run the daily chores, for instance.[3]

The social upheavals, however, are carefully left out. The power shortage and the traffic snarls are the only menaces that Feluda has to deal with in the city. Thus, the city-in-text turns into a cultural imaginary that readers, unaware of the goings on in West Bengal circa 1965, have hardly any problem negotiating with.

The manner of the crimes and Feluda's mode of investigation do not need him to engage with the larger frame of the society in the way his famous predecessor Byomkesh Bakshi used to do. The world of Feluda is unidimensional. The stories, in sync with

---

3 The servants are rather fortunate to have at least a presence in the enormously closed world of Feluda. They even have cameos in the narrative that hardly allows any person, other than whomever Feluda engages with, to exist. In the strictly homo-social space (except only a few, like *Ambar Sen Antordhan Rahasya*) that these stories inhabit, the (male) servants continue to replace the female characters likely to be there in a household. They fit in perfectly with the old, feudal ambience of the (male) clients Feluda would visit. And, lest one forgets, there is a servant in Feluda's residence also: Srinath.

the whodunit tradition, typically end with a congregation of all the principal characters, so that Feluda can explain his deductions step by step and identify the criminal for everyone's benefit. The tradition of the great deductive logic allows Feluda to stage a replica of the courtroom, where the criminal is bodily located by the judiciary and a sentence is passed. In the Feluda stories, both the judiciary and the legal–administrative arm collapse on to the single body space of Feluda himself. He embodies (rather literally) both the prowess of the executive that brings the criminal to book and the ethico-legal power of the judiciary that pronounces the verdict.

Interestingly, the deductive reasoning he deploys with the help of his magajastro (brain-as-weapon) is structurally the top-down logic in which the process of reasoning proceeds from one or more premises to arrive at a conclusion. The certainty here is logically inviolable, since the logic connects premises with conclusions. If the premises are true, the terms are clearly laid out and the rules of the (deductive) game are unerringly adhered to, the conclusion arrived at is necessarily true.

The process is visibly a reductive one. Reaching a conclusion requires a few indispensable steps. First, applying general rules that exhaustively embrace a closed field of discourse. Second, narrowing the choice under consideration gradually until only the conclusion is left, thereby ruling out any scope for ambiguity. Feluda, however, takes this reductionism to a level where the criminal, almost abstracted from the societal fabric he lives in, is not just identified with his crime, but reduced to it.[4]

---

4 Compare: 'The sentence of death is absolute. It maintains that one is guilty of one's crime and therefore is subject to death, which can be said to be absolute because, as Heidegger notes, death in itself contains no other possibility, it is that radical impossibility that is *das*

This narrative mode allows the author to manoeuvre without risking negotiating the larger picture. The criminal is operating in a rather claustrophobic world exclusively inhabited by the protagonist(s) of the story. The first-person narrative of the teenage cousin narrator allows the reader only a strictly truncated version of the socio-spatial interactions that the criminal and the detective engage with. Nevertheless, with a neatly etched certainty that befits a fairy tale, the investigation nails the criminal without allowing any moment of *undecidability* to come into play.[5] The crimes are so acrimoniously engineered and the criminal so unilaterally motivated that there can be no slippage of meaning.

Unless the reader is voyeuristic enough to search for peephole(s) in the story – and thereby break the holy textual contract with the author, not to go beyond the lakshmanrekha – there is nothing in the text that will arouse unease with the portrayal of the city. So, once the limitations set by the author himself are duly accommodated, the non-presence of the real, one might argue, does not disturb the flow of the story.

Now what if one foregrounded the question of time vis-à-vis the space of Calcutta? If such a thing is done, the stories of Feluda, more often than not, will be found offering an archaic amalgamation of time and space. It's a Calcutta with certain sections of its history under erasure. History, it has been noted, has

---

Nichts. The sentence is a decision that reduces the person to an object of presence. The person is identified with his crime and is reduced to it, whereas a Derridean democratic subjectivity would suggest that the person is larger than his crime.' (Calcagno, Antonio, *Badiou and Derrida: Politics, Events and Their Time*, Continuum, 2007).

5   *Golokdham Rahasya* is a rare exception where the sleuth, even after locating the killer, decided not to reveal his name. He just made the killer realize that he had cracked the case. Topshe, the cousin narrator, is the only other person who knows the secret.

been a mainstay of Feluda series, yet it has always preferred to leave out the politico-social movements that had been contemporaneous with the years the stories were written. The narrativized reality there is often an impenetrable one, with a particular set of the insignia of the contemporary filtered out or excluded meticulously.

The contours of the exclusion are significant, because these stories are not set in any temporal imaginary. The coordinates of time remain mostly specified. Especially the first few stories of Feluda have narratives that live the time concurrent to its writing. For example, the second one of Feluda's adventures, *Badshahi Angti*, was written in 1966. The story, we gather, plays out in that year too. The villain of the story, Banbehari Chaudhury, says that he had settled down in the city of Lucknow in 1963. And Dr Srivastava, another significant character, says that Chaudhury has been in Lucknow for the past two or three years. Ascertaining the specific year of the goings on in the narrative is a mere calculation: 1966.[6] An analysis of the plot suggests that

---

6   A few years on, Feluda stories have ceased to keep dates in sync with earlier stories. For example, in *Shakuntalar Kanthahaar*, Feluda told police inspector Mr Pandey that he had known Mr Lalmohan Ganguly for the last five to six years. *Shakuntalar Kanthahaar* was written in 1988, while the story that had them introduced, *Sonar Kella*, was written in 1971. However, dates apart, Feluda stories continue to have references contemporaneous with its time of publication, e.g., the rumour of Skylab falling from the sky or enormous power cuts. As for the treatment of time in Feluda stories, Sayandeb Chowdhury has something interesting to offer: 'The trio (Feluda, Topshe and Jatayu) must remain unaged, frozen in a set of notions, because ageing would destroy the narrative regime that Ray would want to construct. For example, ossified in perpetual adolescence, Topshe would be denied access to things and sights beyond what the desire of the author entails him to and would

at least the first few stories are synchronic with the time they were being written.

The third story, *Kailash Choudhuryr Pathor*, written in 1967, is thus probably set in that year too. There is a fair bit of cityscape woven into its narrative – a perfectly sanitized space, with absolutely no sign of the socio-political disorder of the time.

In more ways than one, this particular story is a microcosm of the entire oeuvre of Feluda's exploits. The space is purged of all troubles save the crime that Feluda deals with.

3.

'By the mid-1960s the city had changed very substantially from the one in which Satyajit grew up. First there had been the effects of the war and the Famine, then riots, the loss of East Bengal to Pakistan at Partition and an influx of refugees, followed by the gradual rundown of the city as a port and industrial base…' writes Andrew Robinson while recounting the run-up to Ray's famous Calcutta trilogy. Further:

> By 1966 an economic crisis was ready to boil over. In March a food movement led to raids on grain shops and many deaths through police firings, followed by widespread strikes and student

---

keep reproducing the child in the adolescent. In a similar vein, both Feluda and Jatayu would continue to function as ageless agencies, standing sentient to the right climatic conditions that can reproduce an adolescent gaze not as a factor of age but of vantage. Unageing is hence "unproblematic" in the Feluda canon, because Ray could successfully decouple ageing from its biological imperatives and turn it into a scopic leitmotif, a way of seeing' (Chowdhury, Sayandeb, 'Ageless Hero, Sexless Man: A Possible Prehistory and Three Hypotheses on Satyajit Ray's Feluda', *South Asian Review*, Vol. 36, No. 1, 2015).

unrest. The Communists had already captured the students' union at Presidency College ... and the college was soon drawn into the conflict; in December, Calcutta University had to close for the first time in its 110 years of existence.[7]

The hegemony of the Indian National Congress, hitherto almost unrivalled in West Bengal polity, had begun to come under threat. The Left was gaining strength, quickly ushering in a new political regime in February 1967. The first non-Congress government, named United Front – comprising the pro-Moscow Communist Party of India, the Communist Party of India (Marxist) and a breakaway faction from the Congress – was sworn into power. The months that followed led to the historic skirmish between villagers and the police in a hamlet called Naxalbari. A policeman was killed, and in retaliation, nine villagers were gunned down, triggering a wave of events that were to have a metamorphic impression on the lexicon of (armed) revolution in India. The spatial repercussion of the unrest didn't take long to reach the capital (and virtually the only) city of West Bengal.

The students had already been upset with the existing system. A Union home ministry review (December 1965) noted that 'student indiscipline' was on a steep and alarming rise. The reasons it listed are significant: (1) lack of proper academic ambience; (2) absence of respect for authority: parental, educational and governmental; (3) ideological dissatisfaction; (4) political indifference. Added to these was the severe dearth of suitable employment opportunities. Not very unexpectedly, then, incidences of student agitation jumped from 271 in 1965 to 607 in 1966, with 42 per cent of the cases taking a violent turn.[8]

---

7   Robinson, Andrew, *Satyajit Ray: The Inner Eye – The Biography of a Master Film-Maker*, I.B. Tauris & Co. Ltd, 2004.

8   Banerjee, Sumanta, 'The Urban Scene', *In the Wake of Naxalbari*, Kolkata: Sahitya Sansad, 2009, p. 56.

The city of Calcutta was far from the peaceful one chronicled in the stories of Feluda. So was the larger space of West Bengal. And Satyajit Ray was evidently there – if not in the thick of it, visibly drawn towards the vortex of unrest.

As Andrew Robinson notes:

> Ray rarely mounted a public platform in support of a cause but in 1966 he agreed to lead a huge silent procession in protest at the Government's imprisonment of demonstrators without trial during the food movement, when many others were afraid to speak out. 'At every such moment you can rely on him to do the right thing, without rhetoric. This is something I find admirable. He needn't do it,' said Utpal Dutta … the next day the Communists set up huge hoardings with Ray's name and appeal printed on them.[9]

Around this time a rally against the Vietnam War in Calcutta saw Ray joining strides with other protesters and reading out an international appeal. Robinson has him reflecting on why he did what he did:

> I would probably have stayed at home, because I'm built differently. But there were so many of my friends involved, I said, 'All right. I'll come.' I believed in what was being done. I wasn't merely assuming an attitude. It's not that. But it is just not me. I don't like taking part in public rallies. I'm very much a private person.[10]

The situation, however, did not allow him to remain so, since by that time the agitating public – to whom he belonged ideologically

---

9 Robinson, Andrew, *Satyajit Ray: The Inner Eye – The Biography of a Master Film-Maker*; pp. 203–04.

10 Ibid., p. 204.

at least – had already turned him into an investment that was widely held to be having an appeal, especially to a vast section of the Bengali middle class across political standpoints. Robinson quotes Utpal Dutta saying, 'One may say that the ruling party lost a lot of its support because Ray had decided to hit.'[11]

The assembly election that followed found the Congress losing to the United Front in 1967. Ray was happy at the result and had high hopes for the new incumbent, Robinson writes, only to be shocked at how the situation had begun to unfold after just a couple of months. The election was in February and in July he wrote to Marie Seton: 'The political situation is getting so rough here that I'm beginning to worry about any Calcutta [film] project.'[12]

It is in this politico-social scenario that Prodosh Chandra Mitter decided to take up the profession of a private investigator.

4.

The modus operandi of detective fiction can be of two basic categories. One that serves to locate the crime (and criminality) as essentially external to the seeker of the *truth*, i.e., the detective. Another that returns the reader back to the originary threshold of meaning and being of the crime and manages to undercut its socially endorsed taxonomy. In other words, it seeks to undermine the distinct categorization of the criminal and the innocent. Clearly, this is not what the stories of Feluda aspire to. Nor is there what Julia Kristeva, in her detective fiction, introduces as the 'proper inquiry'. This is the tool that Kristeva brings in to destabilize the process of othering the criminal.

---

11 Ibid.

12 Ibid.

S.K. Keltner observes:

> The 'proper inquiry' of detective fiction ... engages the subject's identity uncertainties. The quest for meaning can simultaneously challenge and transform the spectacular ego. In this, it differs from the spectacle of detective fiction in so far as the subject comes to recognize impurity, criminality, evil not as distinct from herself or himself – that is, as the Other – but as part and parcel of one's own untenable identity.[13]

While Kristeva tries to foreground the irreducibility of the crime to specific individual/s, in Feluda stories it is perfectly reducible to the criminal detected and bodily located at the end. The technology of the self (of the detective) here is essentially constituted vis-à-vis the other (or the criminal). Jeopardizing this classificatory arrangement would have undercut the moral architecture of the story, scheduled to be published in a children's magazine.

Interestingly, when Feluda stories began to appear in an adult literary magazine a few years later, Ray refused to incorporate materials (and modes) that would befit a crime story meant for the consumption of the adults. He conceded that writing detective stories with things like simple thefts was a huge limitation, but maintained that Feluda stories would have no adult crime per se. In an interview given around four years before his demise to Sanjib Chattopadhyay, another celebrity litterateur, Ray is ruthlessly candid regarding the positioning of the Feluda stories:

---

13 Keltner, S.K., 'Whodunit? Reading Kristeva with the Help of Detective Fiction', *Kristeva's Fiction* (ed. Beningno Trigo), State University of New York, 2013, pp. 37–38.

Satyajit Ray (hereafter SR): There is a problem, you know. Had I not been compelled to keep the teenage audience in mind, writing Feluda stories would have been a lot easier. Can't help it, you know, I can't wipe out the teenage readers of Feluda, and therefore need to be very careful about the content. I can't afford to write about a wide spectrum of crime. Have to restrict myself to things like simple theft.

Sanjib Chattopadhyay (hereafter SC): You mean something beyond curios, antics, art objects …

SR: Like illicit affairs …

SC: Or sexual violence?

SR: Right. Just can't think of having such things in Feluda. To my mind, this is a huge hindrance for a detective story writer.

SC: A limitation …

SR: Serious limitation, I must say. This is precisely why I've stopped writing Feluda in *Desh* (annual autumn number) every year. Now I write every alternate year.

SC: That is, I presume, for the sake of *Sandesh*.

SR: Not at all. This is because I can't come up with an adequate plot each year.

SC: How about writing a detective story for the adult audience?

SR: I'm afraid that's going to leave my countless teenage fans utterly disappointed.

SC: But they have something for them, don't they?

SR: They do, but they're going to demand an explanation. One story a year means they'll be left high and dry the year I write for adults. Honestly, writing more than one detective story a year is beyond my capability.

SC: No, but the year you write a detective novel for *Desh*, can't you make it an adult one?

SR: In that case, I'm going to be blamed straightaway for not writing a Feluda instead.

SC: Well, that's true. We, adults, do read your Feluda stories in autumn number.

SR: Yes, I know. Whatever I've written so far has been read by people across ages. Not just the children, the adults too.[14]

The conversation is revelatory, making clear that the authorial gaze necessarily involves a rule of exclusion. What he can bring into the narrative is effectively guided (and censured) by what he cannot. Feluda is not permitted to deal with something beyond theft, forgery or solving a riddle. Undeniably, there can well be sexual motivations even behind all these apparently innocent crimes, but the author is determined to weave a charm that is diegetically sexless.

5.

Nonetheless, the crime record of 1967 shows Feluda had good reason for turning pro, since there had been an upsurge in the sort of crimes that he was destined to deal with – both in the larger space of India, and in West Bengal. A closer look at the figures can dig out some interesting facts.

---

14 *Desh*, Vol. 18, No. 4, 1987, p. 37. (tr. by the author).

Table 1 shows the upwardly mobile trend of all types of cognizable offences in the country. As the dossier records: 'During the year under review (1967), a total number of 881,981 cases of cognizable offences (under the Indian Penal Code) were reported in India as against 794,733 during 1966, recording an increase of 11 per cent over the previous year.'[15]

Table 1
Total Crime and Rate of Crime: India 1962–67

Year	Population (million)	Total cognizable crime	Rate of Crime per 100,000 population
1962	453.1	674,466	148.9
1963	459.1	658,830	143.5
1964	475.2	759,013	159.6
1965	486.9	751,615	154.4
1966	498.7	794,733	159.4
1967	511.3	881,981	172.5

In 1967, the rate of crime per 100,000 population in the country was, as the table shows, 172.5. However, the figure under the same head in West Bengal was 203.8 and in Calcutta 427.5.[16] If this set of data is not encouraging enough for the young Prodosh Chandra Mitter to switch his profession, there are still other things to support his decision. The following data (Figure 1) show the percentage segments of different types of total cognizable crime committed in 1967.[17]

15 *Crime in India: 1967*, National Crime Records Bureau, p. 5.

16 Ibid., Appendices, p. 60.

17 Ibid., p. 8.

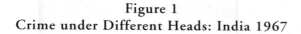

Figure 1
Crime under Different Heads: India 1967

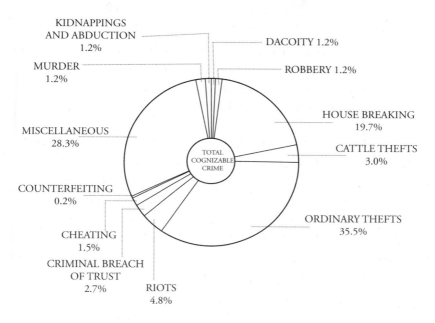

Clearly, there was an upsurge in the types of crime originally earmarked for Feluda. The graphs of those specific types of crime were quite high in West Bengal too. As the record shows:

Thefts Ordinary: Almost all the states registered significant increase in this crime. Overall increase was of the order of 14.1 per cent while the state of West Bengal indicated an increase which is as high as 29.2 per cent. UP and Bihar showed an increase of 22.7 per cent and 24.7 per cent respectively. The crime is very prominent in big cities. Barring Ahmedabad, all others (sic) cities indicated significant increase over the previous year.

Criminal breach of trust: West Bengal has reported a very sharp increase of 48.4 per cent over the previous year.

Cheating: The states of Madhya Pradesh, Maharashtra, UP and West Bengal contributed significantly to the total incidence of this crime reported in the country during the year – approximately 57.0 per cent.

Counterfeiting: This crime has indicated a very sharp increase of 115.7 per cent during the year over 1966 ... Almost all the states have registered a significant increase in this crime during the year as compared to 1966.[18]

The data lead us to another interesting aspect that deserves to be mentioned. Along with the upsurge in the number of crime, a huge number of cases did remain unsolved as well (Table 2). Despite due investigation, more than the half (6,939) of the total true cases (13,052) in Calcutta could not be resolved. The situation was even bleaker in West Bengal. Nearly 70 per cent of the total true cases, i.e., 41,833 of 62,892 cases remained unsolved.[19]

Table 2
Break-up of Cases under Different Categories, 1967

	West Bengal	Calcutta
Cases pending investigation from previous year	12,897	600
Cases reported during the year	84,449	13,185
Cases pending investigation at the end of the year	20,264	437
Total true cases	62,892	13,052
Cases not detected	41,833	6,939

18 Ibid.

19 Ibid.

Feluda could not have asked for a better time to appear as a private investigator. The huge number of undetected cases would likely have dented people's faith in the police and administrative system. Yet, Ray never had Feluda uttering invectives against the police, let alone making fun of them.[20] On the contrary, he maintains cordial relations with the state machinery to counter the criminals. The police in return – with only a handful of exceptions – do not question his credibility and/or capability. Even if they have some doubt, they've allowed him to proceed in his own way. And, in a number of cases, they act just as Feluda has wanted them to.[21]

The state power, in this way, has been accommodated, albeit it is the non-state agency that is scheduled to come to the fore. One might venture a comparison here with Goopy Gyne and Bagha Byne – two typical non-state actors who are mutually supplementary and end up rescuing the state from a devilish plot. The simultaneous emergence of two singular forces – Feluda as a professional private investigator and Goopy–Bagha as supernaturally powered messiahs – might not be a simple coincidence.

---

20 Sherlock Holmes, whom Feluda mentions as his guru, did not really make fun of Scotland Yard inspector Lestrade either. Back home, there is the Bengali sleuth duo Jayanta–Manik (written by Hemendra Kumar Roy) who keep making fun of the portly police inspector Sundar-babu. However, Ray did not go that way. Instead, he opted for a kind of self-deprecating humour, targeted at the popular writers of crime stories. The third one of the famous troika, Lalmohan Ganguly, had to take the barb.

21 The film *Joi Baba Felunath* has a typical Bollywood-like ending, where the police are allowed to enter the scene only after the hero takes his personal revenge.

The Last Word

The question then is, who are the people who keep appointing Feluda to reveal the truth? It's been widely held – and with good reason – that Feluda's clientele consists of a group of people who are aged, sceptic, at best described as 'citizens of a past world untouched by the disquiet of the time around them'. In various stories, these patriarchs live as recluses, yet enjoy the authority in their private worlds not to opt for police in a time of crisis. For reasons ranging from lack of confidence in the capability of the police to keeping unsavoury secrets confined to the familial circle, they want a private eye to investigate the matter.

These people incarnate a certain past in their own respective ways, both in the way they dress or behave or in the manner they conduct themselves. The problem is usually an unwarranted invasion from the present. Feluda is called to put things back in order. That is to say, to reproduce the status – seeking to reclaim the past rather than to problematize it in the process.

Problematizing the past would have thrown up issues that would be hugely disturbing for these people, living a reclusive life in their respective palatial closets. And no less for the narrative, which is necessarily foreclosed since the author is committed to non-adult themes that will not unsettle the preset moral configuration of the story.

Interestingly, in Feluda stories, the space of the client and that of the criminal mostly collapse into each other. Maganlal Meghraj (*Joi Baba Felunath*) or Mr Gorey (*Bombaiyer Bombete*) are exceptions in that sense, personifying an evil extraneous to the inner space of the client. More often than not, an implosion within digs out the criminal lying hidden inside. Interestingly, the emergence of Feluda in the mid-1960s of the past century coincided with the urban rise of the class that is often termed as the lumpenproletariat.[22] Despite being out there in the city space in huge numbers and being positionally vulnerable to different types of crime, Ray does not have them commit the crimes (either as perpetrator or collaborator) in his stories. This is significant, since they are perceived by the middle-class society as potential doers of the types of wrongs that Ray's Feluda sticks to.

There is one more point to ponder. Can Feluda's clientele be seen as a monolith? It appears they can. As was noted above, they are more aligned to the past than present continuous, 'outside the normative code, oblivious to the prevalent civic currencies of transaction'. And, it has also been argued that it is precisely this alignment that motivates Feluda to take up their cases, even if they are mostly trite in nature.[23]

But can one restrict the clientele of Feluda to the people he works for in these stories? What about the trace of cases that the author prefers to be silent about? They are excluded, but do get mentioned, however briefly, thereby managing to be *in*

---

22 'While those employed in the tertiary sector formed the bulk of the urban employed middle and the lower middle class people, the horde of uneducated unemployed or under employed crowding the pavements or the slums of the cities came to form the lumpenproletariat…' (Banerjee, Sumanta, 'The Urban Scene', *In the Wake of Naxalbari*, p. 39).

23 'Digging deeper, one can see how the regular roster of clientele would be unattractive to Feluda not because the nature of crime would be banal – after all most crimes in the entire series do not go beyond theft and murder – but because Feluda's fondness is for an older clientele desperately seeking salvation in a world outside time. In short, it is not the nature of the crime but the profile of the clientele that draws Feluda's attention' (Chowdhury, Sayandeb, 'Ageless Hero, Sexless Man', p. 121.)

the narrative in an oblique yet indelible way. There are a huge number of cases, mentioned by Topshe himself that he's not written about.[24]

Hypothetically, the stories that remain unsaid might contain things the author has decided not to write about. And the fleeting mentions of such cases by the narrator are a deliberate strategy on the part of the author to construct a hyphenated discursive structure: dividing Feluda-that-is from the Feluda-that-would-have-been.

* * *

Sovan Tarafder is the editor, editoral page of *Ei Samay*, and has been a long-standing scholar of cinema with a degree in film studies from Jadavpur University.

---

24 For example, in *Shakuntalar Kanthahaar*, Topshe writes that Feluda is the numero uno private investigator in Calcutta, bagging seven or eight cases every month that help him earn a decent living. Going by this number, Feluda is bound to have a huge number of cases that have not been narrativized by his cousin.

I Want to Be Topshe: Feluda and the Female Reader

Rochona Majumdar

Ido not have a clear recollection of when it was that I first started reading Feluda novels. What I do remember is that *Sonar Kella* was the first film that I was taken to watch in a movie theatre. I say *taken to watch* because I was a two-year-old toddler at the time. Yet, I do have some memories of *Sonar Kella*. I remember the musical score from the film. I recall running up and down the aisle every time the music came on – to the annoyance of other members in the audience, I am sure. I also remember being dazzled by the image of the golden fortress.

A few years later, once I had graduated from reading the Noddy series by Enid Blyton, my mother introduced me to Bengali comic books. At the time, my reading skills in English were vastly superior to that in Bengali. I was stuck with the Narayan Debnath comics, 'Bantul' and 'Handa Bhoda' for a long time. In retrospect, it was my mother who devised an ingenious scheme to get me started on reading Bengali prose fiction. She was and remains a voracious reader. As a child, I used to badger her to tell me the stories she was reading. While she told me some stories at bedtime, she also made it clear that they did not exhaust the entirety of everything she read. Pushed to share more, her standard response was, 'You cannot tell a detective story, you must read them.' She then gave me *Badshahi Angti*, a slim, colourful book.

I had just graduated to Enid Blyton's Malory Towers and St Clare series. As a pre-teen, my world was populated by the escapades of Darrell Rivers, her best friend Sally, the irascible Gwendolyn Mary Lacey. Insofar as action and adventure were concerned, I was an avid follower of the amateur sleuth Nancy Drew. It is only much later, after I left India, that I realized that Carolyn Keene, the author of the Nancy Drew mysteries, was in fact a collective pseudonym for a host of writers put together by the publisher Edward Stratemeyer. Likewise, I learnt of Enid Blyton's xenophobic leanings much later too. I gradually outgrew my fondness for these books. Not out of political correctness but because I had outgrown them. I still recommend them to other children with fondness. But do I ever return to them? No. Yet that slim volume my mother gave, and then a home-bound volume of Feluda novels – my personal version of 'collected works' as it were – that my brother gifted me when I was returning to Chicago to complete my doctoral dissertation, have been incessantly thumbed through.

My brother inscribed the bound volume with a literal translation of the pronouncements of Sidhu Jyatha, advisor to Feluda and proud owner of a magnificent library that was open to no outsider but the detective. He was the elderly uncle, representative of a character type often imagined in urban Bengali lore: someone with encyclopedic knowledge of everything under the sun. Sidhu Jyatha maintained a massive collection of bound volumes of newspaper cuttings that he pored over from time to time – much like the ideal reader imagined by M.K. Gandhi when he was editor of

The Indian Opinion in South Africa, a figure that Isabel Hofmeyr has written about eloquently in her book *Gandhi's Printing Press*. My brother inscribed on the book, 'I could have done a lot of things but had I done so, many people would be out of work. So I chose not to do anything.' Sidhu Jyatha counselled Felu to always keep the windows of his mind open so that sunlight could stream in and clear any cobwebs that might have accumulated from ignorance or sloth. My brother channelled Sidhu Jyatha as I was embarking on that last, solitary leg of completing my dissertation. I try to abide by that advice to this day.

As the years went on, Feluda and his two sidekicks (whom I will turn to in a moment) ventured to far-off places such as Hong Kong, Kathmandu and London. Perhaps this fact of travelling outside Calcutta to other places in India was a charm of reading Feluda stories. In my early years of reading these books, I travelled with him to Darjeeling, Gangtok, Lucknow, Jaisalmer, Shimla, Delhi, Hazaribagh, Puri and Varanasi. There were also places closer to home such as Darjeeling and the fictive Gosainpur. Reading about their adventures, one learned an astonishing amount about these places. They were by no means a mere catalogue of sights that tourists would frequent. Feluda's credo was that in order to truly savour a place, one had to walk around. Automobiles, though not absent, were by no means the only way to travel. So in Puri, we end up walking through long stretches of the beach, meet little boys who fish in the sea in the early mornings and collect shells to sell to tourists. In Varansi we walk around the old city after dinner and get a taste of the famous Benarasi paan; in Hazaribagh we cross the gurgling brook-like river and visit the Rajrappa and Kali temples; and wandering away from the darbar square in Kathmandu end up in pig alley and encounter LSD smugglers.

It is interesting to note in hindsight that the well-travelled detective did not venture too far south of the Vindhyas. Only two adventures, *Kailashe Kelenkari* and *Bombaiyer Bombete*, were set in Aurangabad, Ellora and Mumbai (then Bombay) respectively. Why did Feluda not venture out to the southern states of Tamil Nadu, Andhra Pradesh, Karnataka and Kerala? Surely there were crimes in these places. Interesting though it may be to find a key to this puzzle, my goal in what follows is more personal.

A key to the sites where Feluda's mysteries were situated is found in Sandip Ray's foreword to the collected works. He notes that most Feluda adventures took place in regions his father knew well through childhood visits and outdoor shooting for his films. For example, Darjeeling, where Feluda first makes his entry into the world as a detective in *Feludar Goendagiri*, was where Ray based his first colour film, *Kanchanjangha*. *Sonar Kella* was written on the basis of Ray's intimate familiarity, acquired during the shooting of his fantasy film *Goopy Gyne Bagha Byne*, with different places in Rajasthan. *Joi Baba Felunath*, the second Feluda story that Ray adapted to the screen, was inspired by Varanasi where *Aparajito* was filmed. Indeed Ray's deep acquaintance with Varanasi – its ghats, by-lanes, light, smells and noises – that is so central to the unfolding of the mystery in the movie has been eloquently chronicled by him in an essay from 1957 entitled 'Extracts from a Banaras Diary'. Recall his fascination for the ghats leading down to the Ganga. 'Set out at 5 a.m. to explore the ghats. Half an hour to sunrise, yet more light than one would have thought, and more activity. The earliest bathers come about 4 a.m., I gather. The pigeons not active yet, but the wrestlers are. Incomparable "atmosphere" … [H]ere, if anywhere, is a truly inspiring setting.'[1]

---

1 Satyajit Ray, 'Extracts from a Banaras Diary', *Our Films, Their Films*, Orient Blackswan, p. 25.

No wonder the ghats featured as a critical site in *Joi Baba Felunath*. Our first introduction to the crook, Machhli Baba, takes place there, and it is from Assi Ghat that we get a glimpse of the magnificent barge belonging to the villain Maganlal Meghraj. In another passage in the same essay, Ray writes, 'Explored the lanes of Bengalitola. Those of Ganesh Mohalla are perhaps the most photogenic. What makes them so? The curves in the lanes, the breaks in the facades of the houses, the pattern created by the doors, windows, railings, verandas, columns … here the light is qualitatively unvarying, and one could pass off a morning shot as an afternoon one.'[2]

Every one of these details is used to great effect in *Joi Baba Felunath*. The haunting darkness of the lane leading up to Maganlal's mansion, the play of light and shadows when the hapless Lalmohan-babu is forced to be the target for the knife thrower who is a part of Maganlal's retinue, the encounter with the little boy Ruku, and finally the sad death of the family artist are communicated with such impact in no small measure due to Ray's intimate familiarity with the built environment of the city.

Ray's films, more specifically his films on Feluda, merit a longer and more sustained analysis that is difficult to undertake in the limited space of this essay. Andrew Robinson's wonderful biography of the film-maker refers to an anecdote in which Soumitra Chatterjee, who essayed the role of Feluda in the two films on the detective directed by Ray, asked him, 'Manik-da, I think you have modelled Feluda on yourself?' Apparently, Ray eventually did admit to the similarity in later years when he said, 'I'm sure there's a lot of me in him but I can't tell you to what extent.' Robinson contended that Feluda and Topshe 'are Bengali descendants of Holmes and Watson, by way of Ray'.

---

2 Ibid., p. 26.

Notwithstanding Ray's fondness for Arthur Conan Doyle's hero, I have never felt entirely persuaded by the comparison. Nor have I managed to figure out the key to why these films, unlike most of Ray's other works, failed to communicate their charms to Western audiences. Maybe there is some truth to Robinson's claims that, used as they are to 'hard-boiled and cynical' thrillers, many Western viewers were likely to find Topshe too 'goody-goody' and 'colourless', or the inimitable Jatayu 'silly instead of comic'.[3]

A longer genealogy of children's literature in Bengali and Satyajit's own literary and artistic links to his grandfather and father, Upendrakishore Roychowdhury and Sukumar Ray respectively, may be the key to understanding the books and their particular grounding in a deep Bengali history. But I do not wish to suggest that this claim is either comprehensive or well researched. So, for now, let me shelve the question of why Feluda did not become a global emblem of sleuthing and confine myself to an analysis of his adventure stories in Bengali.

For the remainder of this piece, what I probe in particular is why the Feluda series makes it so compelling to the female reader? Much like Sherlock Holmes, the fictional English detective whom Feluda himself proclaimed as his guru, or even the earlier Bengali detective created by Sharadindu Bandyopadhyay, Byomkesh Bakshi, Feluda stories are equally popular among male and female readers. But why? My explanation is necessarily personal and subjective. I write as a female reader, nay fan, of Feluda. Put differently, the burden of this exercise is to explore my own fascination for these works.

It should be said at the outset that Feluda stories present a challenge to the feminist-minded reader. Not a single adventure,

---

3 Andrew Robinson, *Satyajit Ray: The Inner Eye*, I.B. Tauris, pp. 231–34.

except for a weak later work, *Shakuntalar Kanthahaar*, features a noteworthy woman character. A weak exception is Nilima Devi in *Chhinnamastar Abishap*, who plays a small role in helping the detective unravel the mystery behind the death of the family patriarch, Mahesh Chaudhuri, by handing over to him an important piece of evidence, a tape recorder. All we are told about her is that she is a beautiful woman, has a stellar memory and is a good cook. There are a handful of grandmothers who feature in other stories such as *Jahangirer Swarnamudra*. But the characters of these elderly women are never as well fleshed out, as are their male counterparts. Compare, for instance, the details we have about the grandfather characters in *Joi Baba Felunath, Tintorretor Jishu*, or *Chhinnamastar Abhishap* with the grandmother in *Jahangirer Swarnamudra*. The men are a formidable lot whose fondness for classical music and opium, hobbies such as stamp collection, or a penchant for maintaining diary entries in the form of complex riddles constitute the backbone of the main plot. The grandmothers, by comparison, are pale characters who fade away into the background. At best we learn a thing or two about their habits – such as an addiction to paan or a dip in the Ganga at dawn. These details are not developed further, as a result of which they never emerge as real players in the mysteries.

Feluda, we are often reminded, is a good-looking man. While Soumitra Chatterjee, who played the detective in the first two Feluda films, looked handsome in that role, the books do not furnish many details about his facial features. All we are told is that he is tall (over 6 feet) and quite lean. He gets deep furrows on his brow when he concentrates deeply. He played cricket in college and practices yoga daily. Sometimes his physical fitness manifests itself in the ease with which he picks up martial arts technique such as Mokkairi in *Bombaiyer Bombete*. He is a master of disguise who could easily pass as a hippie or a sadhu. Aside from smoking his trademark Charminar, Feluda has no other addictions. We never encounter him drinking or doing drugs. Finally, despite his multiple skills and talents, not once does Feluda come across as a figure with any sex appeal. Not once do we hear anyone cajole him to get married. He has no love interest. While the world he inhabits is hetero-normative, the books describe a homosocial, emphatically male space from which women are absent as agents.

Feluda is accompanied in most of his adventures by his two sidekicks, his cousin Topshe and Jatayu, the writer of impossibly themed blockbusters. While Jatayu ranks among the most memorable comic characters in Bengali fiction, Topshe who pens Feluda's adventures is oddly under-defined. It is to the ubiquitous Topshe that I wish to turn by way of offering a provisional and subjective explanation for the female reader's attraction to Feluda stories. My argument is that for the girl/woman reader, Topshe is our point of identification with Feluda's adventures. Let me elaborate.

Let us first briefly consider the question of language. The Bengali author Leela Majumdar, also a relative of Ray's, once made some significant observations about Topshe. Topshe never seems to age. Between 1965 and 1991, the time period covered by Feluda stories, his stated age increases by less than five years. He first came to us as a thirteen-year-old and never crossed the threshold of eighteen. He narrated his first-hand account of the thrilling adventures he was part of with his older and much-loved cousin Feluda and their writer-friend Jatayu – and his prose, according to Majumdar, was that of a young boy of that age group.

Here I beg to differ slightly. There is absolutely nothing in Topshe's prose that marks it out as male. Since my teenage years overlapped roughly with Topshe's, I know from experience that girls like myself who went to a decent English-medium city school spoke exactly like Topshe. My Bengali vocabulary, though not chaste, had more expletives in it. In Presidency College, I came across a new Bengali lingo that is the language of the teenage Bengali boy. Today, songs by bands such as Chandrabindu, novels by Nabarun Bhattacharya and Raghab Bandyopadhyay have memorialized this language for us. Girls were quick to pick up this language upon entering college. It made us feel more grown up and with it, for it was risqué and untamed by convention. As I ventured into the world, however, I outgrew it. When I encounter that vocabulary fleetingly in films by Srijit Mukherji, Suman Mukhopadhyay, or in the songs of certain Bangla bands, they bring back memories of college. I sometimes hear snatches of that language in the Bengali spoken by young Bengali graduate students who have just arrived in Chicago. But the more I listen to it, the clearer it becomes that I never owned that language as my own. I was and remain much more comfortable with Topshe's Bangla – easy, flowing, with an occasional sprinkling of English words but never as colourful (and decidedly male) as that of Bengali college addas. Looking back, I would go so as far as to suggest that a boy who spoke like Topshe was likely to be more popular with 'good' girls. By no means effeminate, there wasn't anything in Topshe's prose that transgressed the boundaries of civility, which also served to make these books into objects that no adult ever frowned upon. It is quite possible that young adults who found Ray's films too restrained and aesthetically sanitized when compared to his fiery, earthy and melodramatic confrère Ritwik Ghatak would outgrow Topshe's prose. But that never happened to me.

Leela Majumdar is spot on in her observation that she found Topshe a little too restrained. She observes that he rarely displayed the unruly energy so common in boys of his age. The only exception is when he is presented with a plateful of delicious food. Then the restraint would slip away. Topshe's comportment and mental make-up constitute my second point. While I do not wish to make this a generalization about all girls of all generations, it is certainly the case that, while I enjoyed the occasional tomboyish prank, I had much more in common with Topshe. Like him, I itched to travel. I longed for an elder such as Feluda who would be teacher, comrade and confidant all at the same time. An elder who would take me away from the rules of family into a world that was about liberty rather than licence. What Majumdar found odd about Topshe was precisely what I found comforting.

We first encounter Topshe in Feluda's debut adventure in Darjeeling. He is thirteen-and-a-half, and initiates the adventure when he follows Rajen-babu, the elderly gentleman who was being threatened by unknown assailants, to his home in Jalpahar. Interestingly, in this first story, Topshe's full name is Tapesh Ranjan Bose. In later works, his surname is changed to Mitra, the same as his cousin Felu. While waiting for a music band to commence their performance on a sunny Sunday morning at the Mall in Darjeeling, Topshe eavesdrops on a conversation between Rajen-babu and his tenant Tinkari-babu, where the former confides the news about the threatening letters. Topshe supplies this information to Feluda. In his own words, 'You were seeking a mysterious occurrence. You told me that your skills of detection had become very sharp after reading a lot of detective fiction.' We could argue that it is Topshe who gently pushes the otherwise housebound Feluda into the world of action and adventure. It is only when he tells him Rajen-babu's story that Feluda ventures out of the hotel room in Darjeeling that he has not left once since arriving at the hill resort. In this and subsequent adventures, it is Topshe's ardent desire to see a new place, or his fervent hope that Feluda be assigned a case, that serves as the trigger of the narrative. In this sense, there is no Feluda without Topshe. Seen thus, Topshe is always the primary agent in all Feluda stories.

Lastly, Topshe's appeal is also because of his gift for communicating with readers. Even though Feluda often cautions Topshe that the adventures of Felu Mittir should not read like travelogues, or gives him tips about the ways in which to retain the suspense of a particular story, the narrative comes to life largely due to Topshe's keen sense of observation. In countless stories, he reproduces for us the peculiarities of dialect and prose of the people they encounter. Ray's filmic realism translates itself into Topshe's fantastic ability to create a literary mise en scène. Further, facial expressions, nervous tics, sidelong glances or deadpan looks, all of these are described in Dickensian detail. They are so effective that particular characters – such as the tiger trainer Karandikar (*Chhinnamastar Abhishap*), or Anantalal Batra (*Joto Kando Kathmandute*) who claims that he has a double, or the fake fortune teller Lakshman Bhattacharya (*Hatyapuri*) to name a few – leap off the pages.

Topshe drinks hot chocolate at the Mall during their Darjeeling holiday, while Felu sips coffee. He is repeatedly cautioned by his father and Feluda to bundle up in sweaters and scarves lest he catch a cold. There are some restrictions on his movements because he is still considered too young. There is nothing about Topshe that marks him out as an adolescent boy. In fact, not in a single adventure following Darjeeling, where Topshe advances through his teenage years, is there even a whiff of a love interest, either towards a man or woman. As he turns fifteen, he too practises yoga with Feluda in the mornings. No identifiably male sport, such as soccer or cricket, for Topshe. The few times that he plays an active role, together with Jatayu, in helping Feluda nab a criminal, he is either tailing an imposter on foot, or chasing him on a bicycle. In other words, nothing in Ray's delineation of Topshe's physical prowess mark him out as male. This is not to suggest that he is effeminate or a reflection of British colonial stereotypes of Bengali effeteness. He is gender neutral – someone who could just as easily serve as a point of identification for a young boy or girl. The strictures on his movements, his joy at being allowed to eat paan, or to stay up late at night, travel with Feluda to places near and far when school is not in session is something that the ordinary, middle-class, educated Bengali girl can easily identify with. The absence of an Irene Adler–like character in Feluda's life suggests by implication that Topshe is freed up of any residual feelings of jealousy or desire. And when the three of them, Feluda, Jatayu and Topshe, share the same bedroom, or a railway compartment, they are always depicted as sleeping on different beds and bunks, without a whiff of sexuality entering these spaces.

Why Ray may have chosen to banish sexuality from Feluda adventures calls for a completely different analysis. In his writings on cinema, he discusses his discomfort about depicting sex on screen in no uncertain terms. Eroticism is not absent from Ray's films, but sex, even when it does appear, is not handled with great finesse. Perhaps his Brahmo upbringing had something to do with it. Be that as it may, the Feluda stories he wrote primarily for children, though he never specified the precise age group, crossed the gender divide effortlessly. Feluda is no Byomkesh. There are no parallels to Satyabati in his adventures. As a result, unlike Ajit who often teases the detective about missing his wife, or responds to the fact of his fatherhood, Topshe remains a gender-neutral storyteller. Neither Feluda nor Jatayu, the two adults in Topshe's novel, world have any romantic or sexual dimension to them. Topshe, therefore, inhabits a zone that is full of adventure but none that holds the threat of sexual harm or charm.

It is also fascinating that Ray never chose to depict Topshe as someone who develops a close bond with the children who feature in Feluda mysteries. Whether it is Mukul in *Sonar Kella* or Ruku in *Joi Baba Felunath*, or even Bibi in *Chhinnamastar Abhishap*,

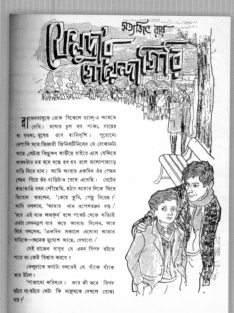

A facsimile reproduction of the first
Feluda story, 'Feludar Goendagiri',
from the pages of *Sandesh*,
December 1965.

Badshahi Angti was first serialized
in *Sandesh* and later published as
a novel.

A facsimile reproduction of the first
page of *Badshahi Angti*, from the pages
of *Sandesh*, where it was serialized
between May 1966 and 1967.

The stories that appeared in *Sandesh*, *Desh* and as novels were illustrated with sketches by Satyajit Ray. This and facing page: some illustrations from *Badshahi Angti*.

Sonar Kella was the first Feluda story to be filmed.
A blockbuster when it released, it has played a pivotal role in
immortalizing the characters and in the growth of the franchise.

Booklet for
the film's India release.

Booklet for
the film's release abroad.

Poster for the film.   Poster for the film.

Title card for the film.

Still from *Sonar Kella*:
Santosh Dutta with
Kamu Mukherjee.

Still from *Sonar Kella*:
The fake Dr Hazra
(Ajoy Banerjee)
with Mukul (Kushal
Chakrabarty).

The camel scene was
one of the memorable
sequences in *Sonar Kella*.

Lobby card, *Sonar Kella*: Soumitra Chatterjee in the climactic camel chase.

Lobby card, *Sonar Kella*: (from L-R) Santosh Dutta (Lalmohan-babu aka Jatayu), Soumitra Chatterjee (Feluda), and the villains, Ajoy Banerjee (Amiyanath Barman) and Kamu Mukherjee (Mandar Bose).

Lobby card, *Sonar Kella*: Soumitra Chatterjee and Siddhartha Chatterjee (Topshe) with Mukul's father who brings the case to the detective.

Satyajit Ray's sketch of Feluda's room in *Sonar Kella*: Feluda, Topshe and Mukul's father are the three characters in the frame. Correlate this with the lobby card in the previous page. One can only marvel at the detailing.

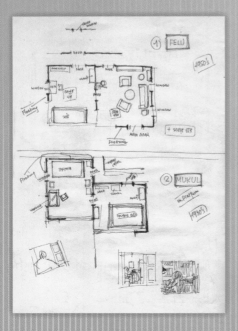

Another set of sketches by Ray for a set in *Sonar Kella*.

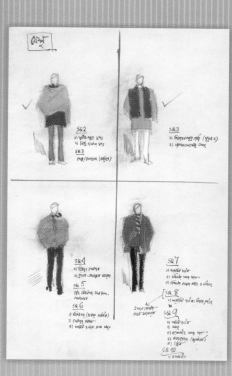

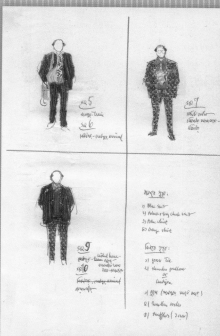

Ray's sketches for the sartorial make-up of Feluda, Topshe and Lalmohan-babu for the film version of *Sonar Kella*.

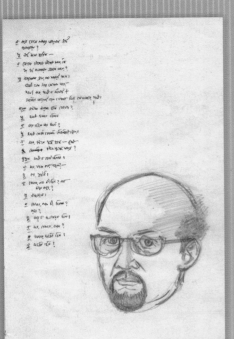

Ray's sketches of
Ajoy Banerjee and
Kamu Mukherjee,
who played the
memorable villains
in *Sonar Kella*.

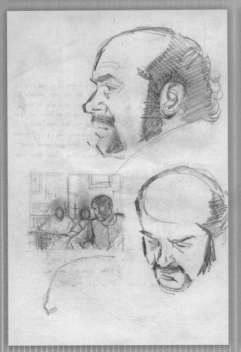

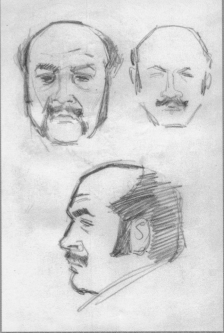

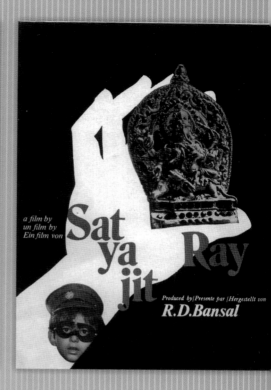

Joi Baba Felunath

The Elephant God • Der Elephanten Gott • L' Elephant Dieu

EASTMANCOLOR

Producer
Produzent
Producteur

R. D. BANSAL

Direction
Regie
Regisseur

SATYAJIT RAY

Feluda returned to the screen five years later with *Joi Baba Felunath*. The film's Indian and foreign promotional booklet covers.

Posters of *Joi Baba Felunath* designed by Ray.

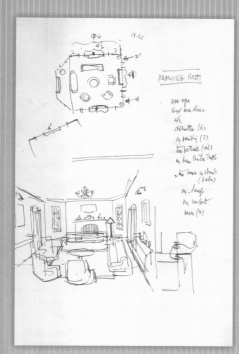

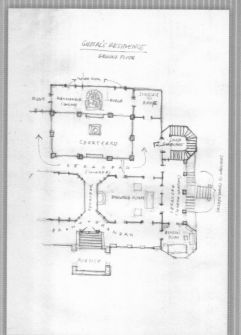

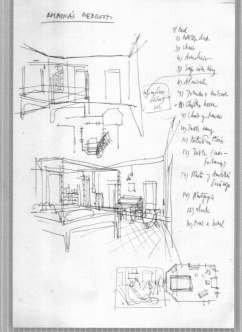

Reproductions from Ray's 'Khero Khata' or storyboard details from *Joi Baba Felunath,* here showing the layout of various sets in the film.

Ray's sketch of the knife-throwing board used in a key sequence of *Joi Baba Felunath*.

Santosh Dutta (Lalmohan-babu) in front of the knife-throwing board in the memorable sequence.

Reproductions from Ray's 'Khero Khata', in which he sketched the storyboard details from *Joi Baba Felunath*.

On location, *Joi Baba Felunath*: Soumitra Chatterjee (in green kurta), Utpal Dutta (next to Soumitra) and Ray (seated, legs stretched) share a light moment.

On location, *Joi Baba Felunath*: Soumitra Chatterjee, Utpal Dutta and Ray. Bijoya Ray can be seen in the foreground.

On location, *Joi Baba Felunath*: Ray explaining a shot as Soumitra Chatterjee and Santosh Dutta look on.

On location, *Joi Baba Felunath*: Soumitra Chatterjee and Satyajit Ray.

Feluda's stories are remarkable for their villains, of which Maganlal Meghraj, immortalized by Utpal Dutta in *Joi Baba Felunath*, is the most memorable.

(Top): Utpal Dutta as Maganlal Meghraj with Biplab Chatterjee as Bikash Singha; (Below): Maganlal Meghraj in his lair, the very essence of evil.

Soumitra Chatterjee and Biplab Chatterjee in *Joi Baba Felunath*.

Soumitra Chatterjee with Siddhartha Chatterjee and Santosh Dutta
in *Joi Baba Felunath*.

On location, *Joi Baba Felunath*: (Left) Ray directs Soumitra Chatterjee;

(Below) Ray is all concentration as he explains a shot.

There was a long hiatus between *Joi Baba Felunath* (1979) and the revival of the franchise in 1996 on screen with Sandip Ray's *Baksha Rahasya*, which was released on TV. In the interim, Sandip Ray made *Kissa Kathmandu Ka*, based on *Joto Kando Kathmandute*, in Hindi for Doordarshan.

(Top): Shashi Kapoor as Feluda, Mohan Agashe as Lalmohan-babu and Utpal Dutta as Maganlal Meghraj.

Sandip Ray had a lot of problems finding producers to revive Feluda on screen. He made a number of stories for television in the meantime. Seen here is a still from a telefilm, starring Sabyasachi Chakrabarty as Feluda, Saswata Chatterjee as Topshe and Bibhu Bhattacharya as Lalmohan-babu.

The franchise took off in a big way with the 2003 film *Bombaiyer Bombete*, directed by Sandip Ray, starring Sabyasachi Chakrabarty as Feluda, Parambrata Chatterjee as Topshe and Bibhu Bhattacharya as Lalmohan-babu.

Poster, *Bombaiyer Bombete*.

Poster, *Bombaiyer Bombete.*

Poster, *Kailashe Kelankari.*

On location, *Kailsahe Kelankari.*

Still, *Kailashe Kelankari.*

 Still, *Kailashe Kelankari.*

Sabyasachi Chakrabarty (Right), Bibhu Bhattacharya (Centre) and Parambrata Chatterjee (Behind Bibhu), *Kailashe Kelankari.*

Sabyasachi as Feluda in *Tintorretor Jishu.*

Sabyasachi Chakrabarty as Feluda, Parambrata Chatterjee as Topshe and Bibhu Bhattacharya as Lalmohan-babu in *Tintorretor Jishu.*

Feluda putting his famed martial arts expertise to use in *Tintorretor Jishu.*

Sabyasachi and Tinnu Anand in *Gorashthane Sabdhan*. Interestingly, Tinnu Anand was an assistant to Satyajit Ray in *Goopy Gyne Bagha Gyne*, before going on to direct Hindi blockbusters with Amitabh Bachchan.

With *Gorasthane Sabdhan*, Saheb Bhattacharya took over from Parambrata as Topshe; seen here with Sabyasachi Chakrabarty as Feluda and Bibhu Bhattacharya as Lalmohan-babu.

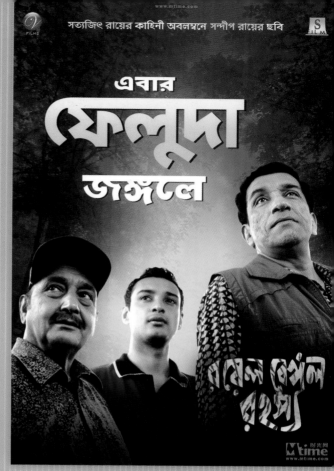

Royal Bengal Rahasya
marked Sabyasachi
Chakrabarty's final outing
as Feluda on-screen.

Sandip Ray has played a stellar role in popularizing the Feluda franchise over the last decade and more. Seen here on location *Royal Bengal Rahasya*.

Sabyasachi Chakrabarty, Bibhu Bhattacharya and Saheb Bhattacharya
in *Royal Bengal Rahasya*.

The Sandip Ray Feluda film has become an important marker of Kolkata's annual cultural calendar. With *Badshahi Angti*, a new actor took over as Feluda. Abir Chatterjee who plays Feluda and Sourav Das, the new Topshe, with Sandip Ray.

it is left to Feluda to charm or win over the confidence of these children. Topshe, therefore, is redeemed from having to play the nurturing role that may have been off-putting to the female reader of Ray's detective fiction. Freed from any gendered expectation, that reader quite likely identifies with Topshe – the recipient of Feluda's knowledge, wisdom and the occasional anxiety. Jatayu too receives his share of attention, but Topshe remains special. In thus being the only claimant of the great Feluda's undivided affection, the presumed beneficiary of the detective's relative financial well-being, his constant companion and student, Topshe is someone that Ray rendered special in these stories. His character is understated: he is only Feluda's 'satellite', not the protagonist. Nonetheless, as the chronicler of his exploits, always privy to the great man's inner thoughts, and leading a life brimming with adventure without transgressing any social norms and boundaries, Topshe strikes a deep chord in female readers. Perhaps many of them, like myself, have often mused 'I want to be Topshe' and returned to Feluda books time and time again.

* * *

Rochona Majumdar is a professor of history and South Asian languages and civilizations at the University of Chicago.

Life Lessons from Feluda

Abhijit Bhaduri

Our family ritual was to go to Calcutta every year. We would take the train from Old Delhi railway station to Howrah station with stacks of Bengali novels for company. Besides the novels, there were stacks of *Desh*, the weekly literary magazine. Every year, just before Durga Puja, *Desh* would bring out an annual compilation that brought together the best of contemporary Bengali literature and made it accessible to masses. It was my introduction to Bengali literature.

Even the weekly version of the magazine had a section on poetry, which is where I discovered Joy Goswami and Purnendu Pattrea and others. There were short stories and serialized novels, where I read the works of Sunil Gangopadhyay, Shirshendu Mukhopadhyay, Shankar, Leela Majumdar, the very best of Bengali literature. That is where I read Pandit Ravi Shankar's autobiography *Raag Anuraag*. *Desh* also carried a section on films and music. Satyajit Ray was often featured, and in multiple sections: in his capacity as director, for the music he composed, or the costumes he had designed. Even as a young boy, I was struck by this man, and his ability to do so many things.

My world view has been shaped in very definite terms by the books written by three generations of the Ray family. My grandparents, who lived in Calcutta, used to send me copies of *Sandesh*, the children's magazine that had been started by Satyajit Ray's grandfather Upendrakishore Roychowdhury in 1913. The very first Bengali book I had read was *Tuntunir Boi* that had been written and illustrated by him. My introduction to the Ramayana and the Mahabharata were through *Chheleder Ramayan* and *Chheleder Mahabharat*. I must have been ten when I read Sukumar Ray's *Abol Tabol* – the last word in Bengali nonsense verse. Then I went on to read *HaJaBaRaLa* and of course the delightful stories of Pagla Dashu. From there, on to the third generation of this family: Satyajit Ray introduced me to the world of Feluda, whose influence has stayed with me over the years.

I met Feluda through the pages of *Sandesh* in 1965. It was his first adventure, called *Feludar Goendagiri* and set in Darjeeling, clearly Ray's favourite holiday destination. His first original screenplay, *Kanchanjangha*, was also set there. But for Feluda fans, Darjeeling is special because it is the setting for his first story.

Fans will all reel off these details. Prodosh C. Mitter is better known as Feluda. He was twenty-seven at the time of the first adventure, *Feludar Goendagiri*. He is 6'2" (Satyajit Ray was 6'4") and is good at cricket (spin bowling to be precise), knows almost a hundred indoor games and several sleight-of-hand tricks using playing cards. He dabbles in hypnotism and is ambidextrous. Has an amazing memory and super-sharp observation skills. His weapon of choice is Colt .32 that is rarely fired. His martial arts training and lightning-fast reflexes come in handy when he deals with the villains. He can draw portraits. A man of few words, he takes notes in his diary and then withdraws to reflect and think through the case. Even his assistant knows better than to disturb him then.

Feluda's first adventure is narrated through the eyes of the thirteen-year-old Tapesh Ranjan Mitra, whom Feluda affectionately calls Topshe. What stayed with me was the illustration by Ray that accompanied the story: the first time I visualized Feluda and Topshe.

I don't know another fictional detective who has such a young narrator-cum-assistant. Young readers identify with Topshe. Feluda then becomes like a virtual mentor, teaching them about the powers of observation and deduction.

There's more still. The novels are also virtual travel guides. Our detective duo are in a new city in every novel, and Ray brings each one to life. Feluda's first adventure was published in 1965–66 and the last one in 1995–96, all set in different parts of India: Darjeeling, Puri, Lucknow, Varanasi, Jodhpur, Jaisalmer and so on. Feluda also travelled abroad to Kathmandu, Hong Kong and London. The descriptions are compellingly vivid. Ray uses historical facts and blends them with trivia and folklore to make each destination come alive.

It is widely believed that Feluda was a stand-in for Ray himself. They certainly had shared passions, like the knowledge of typefaces. Ray created numerous new fonts in Bengali and four Roman fonts as well – Ray Roman, Ray Bizarre, Daphnis and Holiday Script.

In his debut appearance, Feluda used his knowledge of typefaces to start unravelling the mystery. Feluda tells Topshe, 'While Bengali has ten to twelve different typefaces, English has at least two thousand. There are different categories and subcategories among the typefaces.' He refers to the typeface on an envelope and points out that the typeface used there is Garamond. This typeface had originated in the sixteenth century in France, and was so popular in England, Germany, Switzerland and the USA that they started creating their own version of

Garamond. While they all look the same to the naked eye, there are actually minor differences that show up in the different versions of the Garamond typeface, Feluda says.

Feluda looks at the letter that has been written by someone using different words taken from different publications. The threat is mentioned in no uncertain terms: 'Be prepared to be punished for your wrongdoings.' While others are worried about the threat, Feluda observes that the words have been cut using a blade and not a pair of scissors. He says that the words have been taken from different books because the paper and fonts are not consistent. He goes on to add that the words 'punished' and 'prepared' are from a newspaper.

> 'Anandabazar.'
> 'Really?'
> 'Yes. That type is only used in *Anandabazar* – not in other Bengali newspapers. None of the other words have been taken from any old book. Those fonts are barely fifteen or twenty years old ...'

The problem with most fictional detectives is their believability. They are somehow larger than life – and not just because they solve complex crimes and mysteries. Feluda seems approachable and believable. He is the elder brother we all wish we had. Even when Feluda makes fun of his teenaged cousin's naivety, one can see his deep affection for the boy, and how fiercely protective he is. In the debut novel, he coaches Topshe on how to make it easy for the reader to visualize a character. Feluda asks Tapesh to be precise in his descriptions:

> The person who walked was 5'9", fair-skinned, aged around fifty, the hair around his ears had greyed, he had a mole on his chin and was wearing an ash-coloured safari suit. When he walked into the room, there was some hesitation in his demeanour in the way he

cleared his throat, and the way he covers his mouth at that time shows some kind of Western influence.'

This is useful advice not just for Topshe, but for every aspiring writer. Creating characters that are so real that they leap out of the pages of the thriller requires constant honing of that craft. Ray had an advantage. He had mastered the medium of cinema, which has its own unique approach to telling stories. Ray brought in that visual sensibility to his writing.

The best crime fiction has the ability to draw the reader into solving the mystery using the same clues that the detective has. There's a delicate balance here: the detective should always be half a step ahead, but not have any information that the reader does not. That makes it a fair cerebral game between the reader and the author. The dramatis personae have to be numerous enough to keep the reader guessing, but not so many that the reader is overwhelmed. Feluda's stories struck the right balance.

Each adventure would leave me looking at the world a bit more like Feluda. In *Feludar Goendagiri*, Topshe and Feluda are on their way to meet Rajen-babu. He tells Feluda that the house is exactly seventy-seven steps away.

'What if it isn't?'
'It has to be, Feluda. I counted it the last time.'
'Ready for a knuckle punch on your head if you are wrong?'
'Yes – but make it a gentle one. Anything stronger will dislocate my grey cells.'
Strangely, we did not reach Rajen-babu's house in seventy-seven steps. It took an extra twenty-three steps to reach his gate.
Feluda gave me a gentle knuckle punch on my head and said, 'When you counted it the last time, was it while you were returning or going there?'
'On the way back.'

'Idiot! While returning you were coming down a slope. You must have walked down in long strides!'

'Maybe.'

'It has to be so. And that is why you needed lesser steps that time, and needed more this time. Young people need to take long strides when they walk downhill. When you are older, you need to take smaller steps and keep braking on the downward slope – to avoid falling flat on your face.'

These little tips leave the reader just a little wiser. When Topshe is told that the sword used for fencing is called a rapier, he makes a mental note of it and so did I. I identified strongly with Topshe. He had the same anxieties as I did. And then one day, I was older than him, then older than Feluda. But Feluda continued to remain my hero.

I have had the opportunity to work with so many leaders across the world and get a ringside view of their work habits, and I have often wished I could make the adventures of Feluda a must-read for every leader. The best books not only share ideas and advice, but make it easy for the reader to imbibe those lessons.

Take Notes and Reflect

I have seen the most effective leaders across organizations take notes during meetings and then track decisions. Feluda (like Satyajit Ray did over the years) writes his notes in a small diary. As his fans know, the detective has created his own version of encryption by using Greek alphabets to write English words. He does not rely on memory. At the end of the day, he would ask Topshe to recount all the people they had met and some relevant highlights that need to be kept in mind.

The human mind is capable of playing tricks. Take just one example of a cognitive bias – confirmation bias. It is the tendency of people to favour information that confirms their beliefs. One of the similarities that a lot of leaders have with Feluda is that they are all compulsive note takers. They will never go to a meeting without a notebook in which they will write down their observations, their unsolved questions, data that seems to be counter-intuitive. That helps them to track their decisions.

Daniel Kahneman, the Nobel laureate, explains why a notebook maybe the best investment you could make if you wish to improve your decisions. Use it to keep track of what's decided and why. Write down the relevant variables that will govern the outcome, what you expect to happen and why you expect it to happen. You can also write down how you *feel* about the decision and your confidence level in the outcome you expect. It'll also help you distinguish between when you're right for the wrong reasons, and when you're wrong for the right reasons.

While working on a case, Feluda always spends 'alone time' reflecting on what has transpired. He is the quintessential 'introvert'. The popular Myers Briggs Type Indicator (MBTI) does not use introvert to mean someone who avoids social interactions. It actually describes introverts as people who derive their energy from ideas and reflection. They look inwards to recharge themselves and make sense of the world around. MBTI describes 'extraverts' (they spell it with A, not an O) as people who draw their energy from the outside world. To quote the definition: 'People who prefer extraversion draw energy from action: they tend to act, then reflect, then act further. If they are inactive, their motivation tends to decline. To rebuild their energy, extraverts need breaks from time spent in reflection. Conversely, those who prefer introversion "expend" energy through action: they prefer to reflect, then act, then reflect again. To rebuild their energy, introverts need quiet time alone, away from activity.'[1]

---

1 http://www.huffingtonpost.com/2015/08/18/how-introverts-extroverts-communicate_n_7787304.html

Play as a Way to Teach Others

Feluda would very consciously educate his assistant (or satellite, as Topshe described himself) about the history of a place and bring it to life. Sometimes he played word games. In *Badshahi Angti*, he tells his thirteen-year-old assistant that the word 'osteopath' is used to describe a doctor who works with bones. He points out the similarity between the word 'osteo' and the Bengali/ Sanskrit word for bone: osthi/asthi. That sentence opened up a fascination for words that has stayed with me over the years. I too started to keep a lookout for such words. For instance, the word 'widower' and 'vidhava', the Bengali/ Sanskrit word for widow, sound close enough to be related.

Like Topshe, I too learned that the blue scorpion and black widow spider are both poisonous enough to qualify as 'neurotoxic', potent enough to kill a human being. Feluda has the ability to make history come alive. It was in this story that I learnt about the versatile Nawab Wajid Ali Shah of Lucknow who could sing and was also credited with writing the first-ever Western-style opera in India. He composed the thumri *'Jab chhod chale Lucknow nagri, tab haal aadam par kya guzari'* when he was leaving his beloved kingdom after being defeated by the British. Ray used this composition briefly in his film *Shatranj Ke Khiladi*.

In *Kailashe Kelenkari*, Feluda teaches Topshe the mnemonics that he uses to remember numbers. The method is simple – remember the number like an abbreviation. For example, the number 5349 becomes Fi-th-fo-ni.

Some of the most effective teachers blend play with information while teaching complex lessons. One effective method of teaching others is to use a question to arouse the other person's curiosity. Feluda used 'curiosity questions' to trigger Topshe's interest in the subject in every case.

Keep an Open Mind

Feluda meets Lalmohan Ganguly, or 'Jatayu', in *Sonar Kella*, his sixth adventure. The story revolves around an eight-year-old boy who claims to recall living near a golden fort in his previous birth.
Topshe asks Feluda if he believes in parapsychology and rebirth.
Feluda tells Topshe, 'It is foolish to believe or not believe something without evidence. History is full of examples of people who made serious errors because they did not keep an open mind. There was a time when people believed that the earth was flat, you know that, don't you?'
As he investigates the case, Feluda reads up about Rajasthan as well as parapsychology. He reads James Tod's book on Rajasthan, a guidebook on the region, a book on Indian history and two books on parapsychology. Never go unprepared for any meeting. Do your own research.
This is a great life lesson. Successful people will listen patiently to another point of view on a subject. They do not bury dissent. I know the chairman of a very successful corporation who travels economy class in flights to be able to engage in conversations with people unconnected to his business. Once, while travelling, he was seated next to a young entrepreneur, and learnt about his business model. 'When I speak to someone young and inexperienced, they will tell me about the way they see the world. That helps me examine which assumption of mine has become outdated,' he says.

T-shaped Skills

The concept of T-shaped skills, or T-shaped persons, is a metaphor used in job recruitment to describe the abilities of persons in the workforce. The vertical bar of the 'T' represents the depth of related skills and expertise in a single field, whereas the horizontal bar is the ability to collaborate across disciplines with experts in other areas and to apply knowledge in areas of expertise other than one's own.

Feluda's breadth of reading (besides reading *The Statesman* every day) makes him the quintessential T-shaped person. In *Golokdham Rahasya*, a crime is triggered by envy and professional jealousy. Ray introduces the story with Feluda quizzing Topshe about various characters of the Mahabharata.

'Who was Jayadratha?'
'Duryodhan's sister Duhshala's husband.'
'Jarasandha?'
'The king of Magadha.'
'Dhrishtadyumna?'
'Draupadi's brother.'
'Name the conch used by Arjun and Yudhishthir.'
'Arjun's shell was Devdutta and Yudhishthir's conch was called Anantavijaya.'

In *Nayan Rahasya*, Feluda tells us that snakeroot, or sarpagandha, is a species of flowering plant that is useful for treating blood pressure. In *Kailashe Kelenkari*, Feluda is reading *Tintin in Tibet*. Then he goes on to read *The Chariot of the Gods*. He tells Topshe that the Pyramid of Giza has 200,000 blocks of stone, each one weighing fifteen tonnes. He calculates that each pyramid would have taken almost 600 years to complete.

This is exactly the kind of skill that will make a person innovative. Ideas for new businesses often lie in applying the ideas from one discipline to solve the problems in another. Look at ideas from other industries that can be applied to solve problems that are vexing you. Biomimicry or biomimetics is the imitation of the models, systems and elements of nature for the purpose of solving complex human problems.

All too often, people read just what they can immediately use to solve their problem. Innovation lies in our ability to reframe problems by asking interesting questions. If you ask, 'What is the sum of eight and fourteen?', there is only one answer. Reframing it to ask which two numbers can add up to twenty-two throws open a host of possibilities. It is people with T-shaped skills who can find unconventional solutions to problems.

Like Feluda would advise Topshe, we could simply ask, 'How would someone else view this problem?' Maybe ask yourself a hypothetical question by creating different scenarios. 'How would Google solve this problem?', 'How would Disney handle this?', 'How would Feluda solve this? What would he notice that others have not?'

We don't know what we don't know. Reading Feluda is a good starting point.

Seek a Mentor

One of the most fascinating characters in the series is Siddheshwar Basu alias Sidhu Jyatha, the human equivalent of Wikipedia. Sidhu Jyatha is supposed to have made and lost a lot of money doing various kinds of businesses. He now leads a retired life where he plays word games, reads plenty of books, especially books on chess, practises chess moves and constantly experiments. In *Kailashe Kelenkari* we learn that he has the habit of asking rhetorical questions as he smokes his cheroot. He has three almirahs full of books on every possible subject. Half the books are on art – a subject Sidhu Jyatha is passionate about.

Sidhu Jyatha has extensive knowledge of current and historical affairs. He is said to have a 'photographic memory', and is a vast repository of information that comes in handy when Feluda is in need of some. Sidhu Jyatha's vast knowledge comes from a massive collection of newspaper clippings which he has accumulated over the years.

He advises Feluda to read up about the history of criminal investigation. 'If you know the history of the field of work you choose to specialize in, you not only feel more confident, you also find your work more enjoyable.' That is profound career advice. As a human resources professional, I marvel at Sidhu Jyatha's insight – as relevant today as it was when he gave it to Feluda.

Then Sidhu Jyatha goes on to quiz Feluda. 'Who discovered this method of going after criminals by following their fingerprints?' It was not Alphonse Bertillon as most people would say but Juan Vucetich, the Argentine who advocated the use of thumb impressions. He divided the thumb impression into four categories. But it was Sir Edward Henry who refined the system further in the nineteenth century.

Feluda considers Sherlock Holmes to be the numero uno in his profession. When he goes to London, he makes it a point to stop in front of 221B Baker Street, and says that a trip to London would be incomplete if he didn't stop to pay his respects to Conan Doyle's creation.

Create a Compelling Vision

Feluda adventures are all set in different places. In *Badshahi Angti*, Topshe expresses his disappointment when he learns that they will not be going to Darjeeling or Puri, their usual vacation destination (something they shared with Satyajit Ray as well). Feluda creates a compelling vision of Lucknow for Topshe.

Feluda tells him about the splendour of the Bhulbhulaiya inside the Imambara, built more than 200 years ago by Nawab Asafud-daula. Topshe learns that the Imambara has one of the largest darbar halls. The maze was used by the nawab and his consorts to play hide-and-seek, and is the setting for much of the action in the story. Then Feluda goes on to pique the fourteen-year-old's imagination by telling him about the bullet and cannonball marks that are seen on the walls of the Residency, the bastion of the British soldiers during the Sepoy Mutiny of 1857. It is Feluda who draws attention to the curious mix of English and Urdu in the name of Kaiser Bagh, another tourist attraction of Lucknow. He says that Lucknow was called Lakhnavati during the days of the Ramayana.

Countless Bengali tourists have been flocking to the Jaisalmer fort ever since we saw a glimpse of its massive yellow sandstone walls which fade to honey-gold as the sun sets in *Sonar Kella*. Even the locals refer to the fort as 'sone ka qila after' Feluda's adventure.

When Feluda goes to Varanasi in *Joi Baba Felunath*, he makes the city come alive. He asks Topshe if he would consider living in Varanasi for the rest of his life. Topshe thinks for a moment and says, 'Probably not.'

Feluda says, 'What you are looking at is not just a road. You are looking at a road in Benares. Benares! Kashi! Varanasi! That's something. The oldest city in the world, a place of pilgrimage and worship! The city has a kind of magic that is created by a combination of the Ramayana, Mahabharata, sages, yogis, Hindus, Muslims, Buddhists, Jains, all of which come together to make the city rise above the dirt and squalor. Those who live here are so caught up in their daily struggles that they do not have time to look at the dirt. Those who come for a few days cannot think beyond.'

Leaders would do well to learn this lesson from Feluda. It is easier to get people to give their best when they are pulled towards a goal that they are excited about rather than something that they are forced to do. If the vision is exciting and compelling, people will go above and beyond the call of duty. When organizations work hard to measure the engagement levels of the employee, Feluda would advise them to check if each one sees the possibilities and vision that the leader has drawn up. Maybe it is worth looking at how to articulate the vision in a language that the average employee is excited by.

The thirty-five adventures of Feluda appeared between 1965–66 and 1995–96. I grew up in a world where there is no problem that Feluda cannot solve. There is no answer that stumps Sidhu Jyatha. Topshe was the most eager of learners, and tries to anticipate what he could do to contribute to the case and absorb Feluda's methods like a sponge.

All this leads me to say that while Feluda offered me life lessons, it may be time for some succession planning, in the way organizations do. A lot of things have happened. While Sidhu Jyatha may not be around, we now have the Internet. Google News can pull up all kinds of information, and numerous sites like Flickr and YouTube have come up that makes travel redundant in the context of an investigation. Posting a query on Facebook could get you information much faster than taking a trip to a remote location. It is easy to interview people on Skype. If Topshe wanted to connect to an expert on Twitter, it would be infinitely easy. I am not sure if Topshe was inspired enough to want to be a private investigator like Feluda.

With new technology, the role of the detective is also changing. Maybe it is time to get Topshe into the driver's seat and have Feluda navigate instead. Maybe it is time for Topshe to implement those life lessons actively and let Feluda continue to mentor him.

* * *

Abhijit Bhaduri works as the chief learning officer of Wipro and is one of the most influential leaders on social media. His website abhijitbhaduri.com is widely read. He is the author of *Don't Hire the Best* – a book that tells us how to hire for fit with the culture. He has authored two popular works of fiction, *Mediocre but Arrogant* and *Married but Available*.

Do I Love Him or Hate Him? Dealing with Prodosh C. Mitter and His Future

Mir

Do I dare to dislike Prodosh C. Mitter? Oops. Can I as a Bengali? Can any Bengali ever say this openly?

(Crash! Boom! Bang! Piece over.)

Why, you ask? Now I'll happily admit that I am the weirdest of explainers, but bear with me as I take you through la philosophie de Feluda.

First things first. If you have a wife, you know how a detective operates … And if there is also a mother-in-law in the vicinity, you may as well have all of Scotland Yard grilling you.

On that sexist train of thought, I may as well comment on (and acknowledge) the powerful olfactory systems of the women around us. If you are guilty – as men so often are – you can bet your life you will be smelled out.

(Say 'Ah Men!' to that, shall we?)

Now that makes you wonder why writers haven't been writing up a storm of female sleuths. Globally, a Miss Marple or a Modesty Blaise is a rarity. In India, they are practically non-existent.

Although I guess Bengalis might find some comfort in the late Suchitra Bhattacharya's Mitin Mashi. But that's about it. And she never quite got ahead of her male competitors. Shall we look at those noble men then?

The first name I invoke is that of Hemendra Kumar Roy (1888–1963), often credited (not without controversy though) with creating one of the first detectives in Bengali literature. The immensely popular (in his times) Jayanta–Manik tales had – not unlike the Feluda stories – three protagonists: the detective Jayanta, his assistant Manik and a police inspector called Sunder-babu.

But it was way before him when you had Panchkori Dey (1873–1945) and his desi Holmes–Watson team of Debendrabijoy and Arindam. Dey-babu is often credited with the honour of being the first Bengali translator of Sir Arthur Conan Doyle's Sherlock Holmes stories, which were eagerly lapped up at that time.

Even before him came a certain Priyanath Mukherjee and his enormously successful detective and suspense stories. In fact, Mukherjee's writings are often considered to be Bengal's earliest goenda kahini.

But let's return to Hemendra Kumar Roy. His stories were most voraciously consumed by teenagers. And the best part is that his detective was a true-blue Bengali. While most of his predecessors were more interested (and who can fault them?) in creating fiction loosely based on the internationally famous exploits of Sherlock Holmes, Roy was a departure of sorts. He did not simply copy; he created his own sleuth with mannerisms that were Bengali in a sense.

The basic problem encountered by most writers in the nineteenth century pertained to the creation of the sleuth's personality. How to make the sleuth original and not a mere derivation of Holmes? And no matter how hard you tried, the product somewhere down the line would look like a clone of the pipe-smoking maverick solving cases from in and out of his 221B Baker Street abode across the English Channel.

Which is why, the safer bet for most local (read Bengali) publishers would be to simply credit the source, print the translated lines or at most rope in someone to write them differently in the native language and collectively call them an 'inspired series'. That way, one wouldn't run the risk of having to do anything substandard. That's what makes Hemendra Kumar Roy special because he at least tried to move away from the existing practice of creating yet another Holmes clone.

That said, the true fathers of the serious detective stories in Bengal were Sharadindu Bandyopadhyay with Byomkesh, Nihar Ranjan Gupta with Kiriti and, of course, Satyajit Ray with Feluda.

Beginning of a Love and Hate Relationship

My very ordinary middle-class, pre-teen years were mostly spent in a house lodged inside a narrow by-lane somewhere in the heart of the city. In those days, I really didn't have too many modes of recreation. Television, hardly. Mostly the radio. I used to hate the fact that I would have to visit a neighbour to watch *Buniyaad*, *Nukkad*, *Yeh Jo Hai Zindagi*, and the other tele-dramas of the time. I dreaded the '*Chalo niklo … khatam ho gaya … Ab ghar jaao sab*' order from my friends' mothers and harangued my parents about why we didn't own a television. As you can imagine, a visit to the movie theatre was then nothing short of an Eid. With '*Top of the World*' by the Carpenters blaring in my head, I made my way to Majestic or Crown Cinema on the potholed and tramline-marked Rafi Ahmed Kidwai Road in central Calcutta.

It was better than even my dreams. Watching Amitabh Bachchan or Rajesh Khanna do their thing on the big screen; hot chips and popcorn in that air-conditioned hall … Just the balm a telly-starved soul needed. Nothing could match the charisma of those matinee idols. Until, that is, Feluda arrived on the scene.

I first met the sleuth at the school library. And like most of my friends – who knew only Hardy Boys and Nancy Drew and Famous Five – Ray's detective stories were what sparked off my love for Bengali literature. I must confess here that I also loved Sashthipada Chatterjee's 'Pandav Goenda' series almost as much.

Feluda's *Sonar Kella* in a puja issue of *Sandesh* was first blood. Later on, I caught the blockbuster on a sultry Saturday evening on Doordarshan. And that love affair with Soumitra 'Feluda' Chatterjee took off like a forest on fire. I was addicted to this character. And though he was fictional, there was this constant hope that I might just bump into him in front of some local paan shop lighting a Charminar. Maybe I could see Feluda get off a taxi right in front of me and walk his way inside New Market to buy some fresh chanachur. Or better still, getting freshly ironed clothes from the laundry next door before embarking on his next trip. It was that real. Or should I add, surreal.

I came upon Byomkesh way later when I was in college. I did try reading it during my school days but, like many others, found it difficult to comprehend. The language was dense, and the themes too complex.

But with Feluda, it was an I-know-you-very-well zone I shared with no one else.

Oh, but I began this piece with the disclaimer that I dislike Mr Mitter. Now, am I not contradicting myself?

Perhaps not. Let me tell you why.

If I were to think about it, I'd say the radio had something to do with this dislike. More specifically, the storytelling of *Sunday Suspense* on FM radio – a revolutionary experiment far removed from its ancestor, AIR. In *Sunday Suspense*, we created audio versions of the most popular detective dramas and, as was expected, the biggest hits were the Feluda stories. The first show was aired almost three years ago and the programme remains one of the most tuned into ones in Bengal ever since.

But the journey hasn't been easy. FM's popularity was driven by its crystal-clear sound and music that was contemporary and fast-changing. How could one expect people to be patient with storytelling in the middle of all that roil? It was a menacing world, and remotes and the ability to switch off content the moment it bores the listener were only part of the new threat. The battle lines were drawn between competitors. Taking a risk that big was impractical. But Radio Mirchi still produced *Sunday Suspense*, and the show continues to have listeners all these years later.

The audiences were hooked, and we embarked on a beg-borrow-steal mission. Beg, borrow or steal from literature across the shores to characters closer home.

Choose an existing story that has dollops of mystery. Lay out a sound garden across the plot. Get killer voices on board – with the best of them voicing the detective.

Easier said than done.

And this is why I dislike Prodosh C. Mitter.

I have longed to be the voice of a detective in an audio drama.

With the backing of a superb team, I recorded both Byomkesh and Holmes. It was a stupendous experience. Unmatched since.

But Feluda was not meant for me.

Enter Benu-da aka Sabyasachi Chakrabarty

The radio station I work with has long been a part of Sandip Ray's promotional plans for his Feluda blockbusters. And during these promotionals I've always found Sabyasachi Chakrabarty being bombarded with expectations of epic proportions. One of Bengal's most talented actors, Chakrabarty has faced constant – often ruthless – comparisons with Maestro Manik's choice, Soumitra Chatterjee.

Brand Feluda inspires that kind of passion. He is a fictional character who is more corporeal (in the Bengali imagination) than the actor playing him. Consider this: Soumitra Chatterjee acted in only two Feluda movies. But the shadow of those films loomed over what is perhaps the most sterling career in Indian/ Bengali cinema.

Chakrabarty knew this was coming, and that kept him on his toes. 'I'm going to do it my way,' he said, and the new franchise gradually brought in a new age of Feluda movies. I still remember the session I had with him on Christmas Eve 2011. *Royal Bengal Rahasya* had released just the previous evening and the social media was abuzz with self-styled critics mocking the actor with ruthless comments like 'Feluda naaki Felu kaku?'

In three years, the actor would be replaced by a younger and fitter substitute, and his successor (Abir Chatterjee, who was already doing Byomkesh with another celebrated director) would face similar comparisons. Then again, the media was just doing its job.

To return to the Feluda adventures on radio, Chakrabarty was the obvious choice for it. His baritone and the fact that he was already playing the sleuth in junior Ray's movies made our project that much stronger.

Chakrabarty reread all of the stories, reinventing himself to do justice to the character. Sort of reincarnation, one might say.

I heard him telling the director of the series, '*Golpota besh koyek baar bhaalo kore pore nile* better *hoto … taarpor* recording-*e jetaam.*' I was taken aback for a bit, but then realized how important it is for an actor to get into the skin of the character. Even if it's for an audio play. Even more so if the character is one of the most iconic characters in a cultural landscape – from Feluda to the low-key

Topshe to the loveable goof-bag Jatayu, and indeed the villains, whether it is Maganlal Meghraj or Mandar Bose, and even walk-on characters like that hard-to-please boarder at the Calcutta Lodge (in *Joi Baba Felunath*).

Now when you're playing out these characters on radio, the task becomes both challenging and interesting. How do you use a soundscape to bring a character to life when you hear Soumitra Chatterjee often comment on how he would use his eyes to bring Feluda to life?

Feluda was then fortunate to find a voice that matches gravity with elegance. Like Sabyasachi Chakrabarty's.

Meanwhile, I hit upon a realization of my own. A fictional character can make you feel diminutive. Just the weight of his charisma was too much.

I realized that I was not the right person to voice Feluda. Why, you ask? How is it different from playing a Byomkesh or a Holmes? Honestly, I don't know. But I have not had the courage to attempt a Feluda.

Perhaps for the first time I realized that I was lacking in many respects when it came to essaying the voice of the man on air. If someone were to question me about what's different about playing a Byomkesh or a Holmes and a Feluda on air, I would still be searching for an answer. I have found myself voicing so many other characters in the stories. But never had the courage to attempt a Feluda. It is just too daunting. It is actually beyond my sense of perception to explain the ingredients required for being the voice of Feluda on radio. Will I ever do it? Rather, can I ever muster the courage to do it? Honestly, I don't know. Maybe yes or maybe not. For the moment, however, it is best to listen to Sabyasachi and enjoy the other characters that I have lent my voice to. After all, they make the stories as much as Feluda and I am glad to have been part of the oeuvre.

So I pause and wonder how the actors who portray Feluda on screen prepare themselves for the guillotine. Because no matter how many times you face the media and say stuff like 'I don't believe in looking back' and 'I'm not influenced at all by what's been done before me', there is no escaping the original team of the creator and his Feluda.

Half a Century Later

Through five decades of his existence, Feluda has resisted modernization. True, in Sandip Ray's films, there is some honest contemporization, but these changes are by and large cosmetic.

If we look at the Sherlock Holmes stories, in adaptations on television, the big screen, stage and radio, more than ninety actors have played the detective since the beginning of the twentieth century. A gentleman called Basil Rathbone portrayed Holmes in as many as twenty films and plays between the late 1930s and the mid-1950s. That's a record by itself. But to my friends and me, growing up in the 1970s and '80s, Jeremy Brett was Holmes personified. Brett would just hold you by the collar and have you follow the trail of the mystery like a bloodthirsty hound even if your ancestors had nothing to do with the Baskervilles. With all due respect, a Robert Downey Jr or a Benedict Cumberbatch could do with lessons from the man.

That's what I think anyway. If I were to ask people around me, no single Holmes would get a clear majority. I'd like to think Brett stands the best chance. But the point I'm making here is that it is the stories and the plots that continue to capture fan imagination. Whoever plays Sherlock – from Brett to Lee Miller – will inevitably attract instant attention. The cult is such that people will watch and also, soon enough, they will criticize. The passion for these characters is such that they provoke charged reactions.

Likewise, Ian Fleming's James Bond continues to set the box office afire irrespective of who is playing him – barring a George Lazenby, I guess. Look at Sean Connery (undoubtedly the most prolific 007 on screen) or Roger Moore or Pierce Brosnan play Bond or, more recently, Daniel Craig, and you see the power of a brand that has endured for six decades and counting. So much so that Craig has recently spoken of the difficulties in playing Bond because of the superhero cult associated with the character.

Add to that, the Superman-Batman-Spiderman (and other superhero) barrage of movies. Hollywood has not only maintained a tradition of gloriously recreating literature on celluloid, it has also upgraded the promotional tools in keeping with the times. From memorabilia to souvenirs to theme parks ... the publicity machine serves to grow the belief, or feeling, that these men of mystery and intrigue actually exist and are very much part of our everyday lives whether we like it or not.

They have not only taken their stories to the next level, they have also marketed their products like they were selling an actor of repute in the international bazaar. Yes, sometimes the exercise is very in-your-face but then that's exactly how they have grown into gigantic proportions and that's the method they have painstakingly developed to take their products to alien shores where they've been customized to suit the demands of the host, often non-English-speaking nation. The language barrier has ceased to exist in most cases. So whether it's a detective character or a cartoon (Disney and Marvel being the kings in this sector), the product goes viral worldwide. Almost instantly. And now with digital platform opening up, even the sky is not the limit for such fascinating endeavours.

Lessons Waiting to Be Learned

Here let us take stock. We have great content in Feluda. We are actually in possession of a treasure trove waiting to be explored further. In order to transform the character into a national phenomenon (talking global would perhaps be a bit too ambitious at this point), we could strategically apply so many of our resources. It just requires a masterplan and the vision.

Nothing will survive the digital invasion (call it 'onslaught'). Music and musicians have been thrashed left, right and centre. Not just the type of music but also the methods of sampling have completely changed. Those who have resisted on grounds of ethnicity and aesthetics have been bulldozed multiple times over. The fact that the music industry is bleeding points several fingers at systems that could have been reformed, situations that could have been pre-empted, decisions that could have been taken well in advance. Piracy today is not an unfortunate curse. It's actually a by-product of our mediocrity that stalled or rather throttled the music companies one by one. Everybody saw the flood coming, but nobody stood up to build the dam.

Had Feluda been walking the streets of Kolkata in flesh and bones, his blood would have stoically whispered, '*Byapar ta bhaalo thekchhe naa re,* Topshe.' (Things are not quite fine, Topshe.) And that's because the gene of that character is so progressive. While leafing through his escapades, you get that huge sense of propriety that this man belongs to you and your family… and here is one man who just cannot go wrong. He never miscalculates, never misjudges his opponent, no matter how cunning the villain is. He is always in touch with the current and contemporary. And he seeks the truth without being impractical or loud in any way.

So, let's make some more noise about the man, who in real life would have perhaps preferred to be very discreet. Heavy-duty merchandise. Feluda on T-shirts, Feluda on banners and streamers, sippers, coffee mugs ... Online games with the animated Feluda shooting at his opponents. Comic strips. Audio books. Documentaries ... the works! Let's not stagnate with the comforting thought that Sandip Ray will be generous and gift us a film on Christmas every year. There is so much more to be done. In fact, there is so much more *we* can make Feluda do.

Bengalis face a lot of flak for not being enterprising enough, for being laid-back and for losing that cutting edge that separates the brilliant from the 'just being there'. The confidence that Feluda can never lose to anything or anyone is something we Bengalis need as a tonic. A tonic that can cure you of all your prejudices, your worst fears ... a magic potion that somehow makes you believe that when you ring that doorbell at his 21 Rajani Sen Road residence in Ballygunge, you will find a young lad called Topshe answering the door, courteously ushering you into the drawing room, seating you comfortably on a wooden sofa, soon to be joined by a 6'2", handsome man in his late twenties, hands folded, doing a polite nomoshkar, welcoming you officially by handing over his visiting card with the words 'PRODOSH C. MITTER, Private Investigator' in neat simple calligraphy and then, after ordering for liquor tea, offering you a Charminar, lighting both yours and his, observing you while gently drawing in the smoke and then finally exhaling with the first words of business: '*Haan ebaar bolun ... Ki korte paari...*' (Yes, tell me, what can I do for you?)

Feluda *shob paare*! Feluda can do anything.

And that's one unshakeable belief we need to protect. Come what may. And at every cost.

* * *

Mir Afsar Ali aka just Mir is a radio jockey, master of ceremonies, television host, actor and singer. With more than 16,000 hours (over a period of twenty-one years) of radio programming experience, Mir is arguably the most popular FM Radio jockey in Bengal and eastern India. Mir is also the lead vocalist of a band called Bandage and has also been presenting his own brand of comedy on a show called *Mirakkel* on Zee Bangla for the last nine years. It has completed eight seasons.

Part Three

'Feluda Is an Out-and-out Entertainer, which Byomkesh Is Not'

Boria Majumdar in Conversation with Soumitra Chatterjee

It is a damp, rainy morning in Kolkata and I am a tad worried I will not be able to make it in time for my meeting, thanks to all the waterlogging. Utterly inappropriate, because Feluda is a stickler for time. My destination isn't 21 Rajani Sen Road, Feluda's house, but Golf Green, where the legendary Soumitra Chatterjee, the first and still the most iconic Feluda, now lives. At close to seventy-six, Chatterjee remains the true Feluda for the discerning fan. Feluda doesn't like small talk, and that is what I am prepared for. When Soumitra Chatterjee answers the bell, I feel every bit like a client seeking justice at Feluda's door. I am there, after all, to request him to unravel what it was like to play Feluda, to be the man who had become Bengal's most loved icon.

In front of me is the man for whom Satyajit Ray was forced to change the illustrations in the Feluda stories. Such was Soumitra's acceptance that, in the aftermath of *Sonar Kella*'s release in 1974, young boys and girls would start shouting 'Feluda, Feluda, Feluda'.

Interestingly, Chatterjee did not like this adulation. If anything, it rather frustrated him. For him, it was a sign that his other work was not being taken seriously. Apu and Gangacharan, he thought, were losing out to Feluda. Nor did he like the fact that Feluda could ever be plump or middle-aged, one of the reasons why he stopped playing the character when Satyajit Ray's son, Sandip, decided to carry the franchise forward. A man of strong opinions, Chatterjee opens up about his engagement with Feluda in what turns out to be a rather long adda.

Where do you locate Feluda in your oeuvre?

To tell you the truth, Felu came to me exactly the way he did in the life of most Bengalis. I had become a fan of Manik-da's detective soon after the publication of *Badshahi Angti*. The pre–*Badshahi Angti* stories, I feel, were rather simple, and no one could have imagined Felu would become the icon that he did in the years to come. But of course, I had never imagined that I would be the one to play the character on screen. When Manik-da first called me to say I would play Felu in *Sonar Kella*, I was thrilled. Felu had an appeal that cut across all age groups despite being a series written primarily for teenagers. I still find it difficult to believe how all Bengalis between eight and eighty had begun to love Felu. At the time *Sonar Kella* was shot, my own children were teenagers and it meant I could finally do something as an actor that they could enjoy. This was a matter of deep personal satisfaction. The nature of the Bengali film industry was such that I hardly got an opportunity to do something for my children, and Feluda was a rare exception in that sense.

I must confess that I had never imagined Felu would become a cult almost overnight after *Sonar Kella*'s release in 1974. The film was such a hit that every time I went out of the house, boys and girls would scream 'Feluda, Feluda' the moment they spotted me.

After a point, this overwhelming adulation began to frustrate me a little. I had a feeling that my other work, Apu in *Apur Sansar* or Gangacharan in *Ashani Sanket*, for example, characters which were as close to me as Felu, were being ignored by the viewers. I started to ask myself if I would be remembered only as Feluda. It was only later that I managed to convince myself saying this wasn't a problem after all. Even if one person remembered me as Feluda, I should feel satisfied and proud. In a way, Feluda did make me universally acceptable across Bengali society.

When you were first told by Satyajit Ray that you would play Feluda in *Sonar Kella*, how did you prepare? Did you want to read the novel one more time, or watch other detective films? Was there any particular detective, like Holmes or Poirot, you watched or tried to draw upon?

No, I did not watch or model myself on any one detective. I was an ardent fan of Conan Doyle and Agatha Christie, and also enjoyed reading Raymond Chandler and George Simenon. But that was even before Ray started writing Feluda. I had also watched most of the Sherlock Holmes films, but my reading of detective stories or watching detective films had nothing to do with playing Feluda on screen. All I did while playing Felu was to follow the script to the best of my ability. I had already read Feluda's adventures multiple times, and did not need to go back to them to understand Felu better. The script, I can tell you, was my bible and that's what I used to follow.

How do you see Byomkesh and Feluda? Many say the Byomkesh stories are far more sophisticated pieces of literature. Would you agree?

Byomkesh is far more serious than Feluda. And yes, the Byomkesh

stories are more nuanced than the Feluda adventures. But the
singular difference between Byomkesh and Felu is that Felu is an
out-and-out entertainer, while Byomkesh is not. Felu's constituency
is universal, Byomkesh's is not. Felu can reach out to every section
of society, but you need to be mature enough to appreciate
Byomkesh. While both search for the truth, Felu does it in a far
more accessible way and has a very different kind of romance
attached to him. While I am by no means trying to suggest that
Byomkesh isn't popular – in fact at one point his popularity was
equal to that of Felu's – his reach is perhaps less than that of Feluda.

**What according to you are the most endearing qualities
of Feluda? What are the messages that Satyajit Ray
wanted to convey through the character?**

The three fundamental traits are integrity, honesty and morality.
Felu is upright and honest. And the other thing, which appealed
to me a great deal, is his patriotism. In both *Joi Baba Felunath*
and *Kailashe Kelenkari*, Feluda's nationalist self is evident. In
Kailashe Kelenkari, he detests the fact that national treasure is being
siphoned off and is even willing to investigate the case at his own
expense. And one must also keep in mind that Feluda is not very
rich. In fact, even when Sidhu Jyatha offers him money to travel to
Ellora, Felu very politely turns him down. Again, in *Felunath*, he
is livid because the Ganesh could have been sold off by Maganlal
to a third party and had every chance of being taken out of India.
While many have criticized Manik-da saying he had deliberately
kept Feluda immune from the contemporary politics of the time,
I'd like to point out that Felu's nationalism and patriotism need to
be studied. It is a very different kind of politics that Ray wanted
Felu to engage with. Felu may have been cocooned from the leftist
politics of the time, but his engagement with other key issues is
no less important.

The other quality that makes Felu a very special person is his loyalty to friends. He is fully committed to Lalmohan-babu, and that's something I thoroughly enjoyed while playing the character. Soon after the knife-throwing scene in *Felunath*, when the three of them are thinking back of what happened, sitting on the banks of the Ganga, Felu says what I will always regard as the best dialogue of the film. He says if he was unable to avenge what happened to Lalmohan-babu, he would leave the profession. '*Ami hoy er badla nebo nahoy goendagiri chhere debo.*' Now these are really strong words, and unless you are deeply committed to the bond of friendship, you can't say it with conviction.

Let me stop you here. So, when you played Feluda in *Felunath*, you actually started to feel what Feluda felt for Lalmohan-babu, and that actually helped you play the character better?

In hindsight, yes. I have always felt that unless you are comfortable with something, you can't portray it well on screen. For example, if someone has never fired a revolver in his life and is suddenly asked to do so in a film, he wouldn't be able to do justice to the scene. The way he holds the revolver, the movements of his hand and his expressions will indicate to the viewer that the actor is not comfortable with what he is doing. In my case, I had been in the National Cadet Corps for six years, and was used to horse riding and shooting. My father had a revolver and on occasions allowed me to hold it. That helped me in *Sonar Kella* when I had to fire my Colt .32.

Again, if I did not feel deeply about what Maganlal did to Lalmohan-babu, I would not have been able to do justice to that scene. If you see the scene, Felu sitting solemnly with a frown on his face and gazing at the Ganga, you know that here is someone who is not in the best frame of mind. It is his deep empathy for his friend (whom he feels he has let down) that prompts him to say he will avenge the insult or will leave the profession. This is one dialogue I will forever be proud of having said as Feluda.

How much of Satyajit Ray do you see in Feluda? Many say Feluda is largely a manifestation of his creator.

To a very large extent, this is the truth. Felu's qualities – morality, integrity and honesty – were qualities that Manik-da was known for. The fact that Feluda is an avid reader, he loves to travel, he is 6 feet tall: this is all true of Satyajit Ray as well. Also, the locations for the stories are all places Manik-da had visited. Darjeeling was one of his favourite places and that's where he shot the classic *Kanchanjangha*. Hence we get *Darjeeling Jomjamat*. He visited Varanasi many times and had filmed *Aparajito* there in 1956. That's where the genesis of *Joi Baba Felunath* lies. Again, he shot *Goopy Gyne Bagha Byne* in Rajasthan and it was in the course of this shoot that he discovered Jaisalmer, the site of *Sonar Kella*.

This fascination for travel is something Feluda too is imbued with, and it is natural that he would read up extensively about the place he is travelling to. When he educates Topshe about a particular place, there is a degree of simplicity to it. That was again something Manik-da was known for. He would not speak much or try to force the issue. Rather, he would communicate things in a simple manner, in a handful of sentences. Manik-da *gyan diten na*. Just *sahaj kore bujhiye diten*. Feluda-*o kakhono* Topshe *ke gyan dey na, bado dada hishebe sahaj kore bujhiye dey.* (Satyajit Ray didn't preach. He explained things simply. Feluda too never preached to Topshe. Rather, as his elder brother, all he would do is explain things to him in an affectionate and accessible manner.)

I even felt that the earliest illustrations of Feluda bore a striking resemblance to Manik-da. In fact, I remember a conversation during which I had mentioned to him that every time I see the illustrations, I feel it is Manik-da himself. Feluda's height, high cheekbones, his build, all to me was Manik-da. Manik-da, however, did not agree. He said that it was commonly believed his Feluda illustrations were modelled on me. I was embarrassed.

For my part, I should tell you that many of the mannerisms that I have used in the film were modelled on Manik-da. The way I tried to speak was exactly the way Manik-da spoke. Take the iconic train scene in *Sonar Kella* when Jatayu first enters the film in Kanpur. Jatayu, like most Bengalis when they leave Kolkata, starts talking in Hindi and it is only when he realizes that Felu and Topshe are Bengalis that he switches to speaking in Bangla. That's when Felu says, '*Apni* Hindi *chaliye jete paren, besh lagchhe.*' (You can continue in Hindi. I am enjoying it.) That one sentence has Manik-da written all over it. Anyone who knew Manik-da well will tell you that's how he spoke. While there was always a degree of self-confidence and sense of assurance, he was never rude or arrogant. Also, he had a very subtle sense of humour that I tried to imbibe while playing Feluda in both *Sonar Kella* and *Joi Baba Felunath*.

Let's talk about *Sonar Kella*. How do you remember the classic?

Needless to say, I have very fond memories of the movie. The high point, however, has to be the entire last sequence, which was shot in a little under four hours and was a work of pure genius. I would like to talk to you at length about that a little later. But the one scene that I remember with both fondness and trepidation is the one involving the scorpion. It was a real scorpion that we had used, and that particular scene was shot in Kolkata. At the time, Kolkata was reeling from power cuts and I remember that, just when the scene was about to be shot, the power went off. The scorpion had been put on the bed next to me and in the dark I had no idea where it might be. Honestly speaking, I was not scared. There was very little that I could do before the lights came on. In fact, I remember thinking that if it did bite me I'd have to bear the pain, for how would we spot the scorpion in the darkness? Once the lights came on, we were all relieved to see the scorpion crawl down the side of the bed on to the floor. That's when it was caught again and put in a bottle. This is the one scene that I can't forget.

To return to that last sequence, I must say I was partly responsible for what Manik-da had to go through. It was winter in Jaisalmer and seriously chilly in the mornings. Besides, the fog was so heavy that we could hardly start shooting before 10 a.m. And after 4 p.m. it was impossible to shoot in the fading light. It so happened that we had to board a train for Jodhpur in the evening on the last day of the shoot and I had to take a connecting flight to Kolkata the following morning. Both Sailen Mukherjee (who played the original Dr Hajra) and I had a stage performance in Kolkata the next day. Tickets had been sold and there was no way we could miss the flight. Our schedules were such that, with just one day in hand, we had the entire last sequence to shoot. In terms of numbers, it would amount to seventy or so shots. Also, in those days, it was extremely difficult to get bulk train reservations overnight, and the size of our unit meant it was improbable. The bottom line was we needed a miracle to finish the film.

The evening before the last day, all Manik-da said was: '*Hoye jabe.*' (It will happen.) Next morning, we had reached the shooting site early and were waiting for the light to improve, so that we could start rolling. I had not seen Manik-da as agitated as he was on that day. He was literally running from one spot to another, and shouting out instructions to unit members. Not once did he consult any papers. The other members of the unit were all confused at what he was doing. But Manik-da, who had a photographic memory, had everything organized in his head. It was just extraordinary to see him in action. He was taking shots himself, and within minutes moving to the next location. I still get goosebumps when I think that, in a little under three-and-a-half hours, we managed to film the entire last sequence of the film. It must be some sort of world record. I was from a film background and that made what was happening in front of my eyes seem all the more incredible. Even in all the haste, Manik-da never gave up his attention to detail. He would shout out the exact height in which he wanted the camera, tell us exactly what he wanted and get things done at lightning speed. When I say his attention to detail, let me give you an example to illustrate the point. This was the scene when Feluda gets the inland letter from Dr Hajra, which has Hajra written with a J. As is well known, it is the spelling that helps him nab the imposter. He understood that the man in Rajasthan was a fraud for he had signed Hazra with a Z. When Ray asked one of the unit members for the inland letter, he was handed a brand-new one. He himself wrote out the letter and that's when he realized that the inland wasn't stamped. 'Stamp *mere ano ni*' (you have not got it stamped), he said and was upset at this very basic mistake. No one from among the unit members said a word because they knew that Ray was unhappy and had reason to be. That's when he asked someone for a black pen. He insisted that the pen should be a black dot pen and not blue. I was intrigued. Soon after, he started drawing the postmark on the inland letter. And in a matter of minutes he had finished the job. It had its broken edges like we often see in a postmark and, unless you were told, it was impossible to figure out that it had been drawn. Just as the shot was being taken, I was itching to find out if Manik-da had got the size right. For that's where he could have gone wrong. To my complete surprise, when I compared the drawing to a real postmark I sensed that he had got it right to the nearest millimetre. This is testimony to his phenomenal memory, something that stood out when he was shooting the last sequence of *Sonar Kella*. While you and I will not even bother to see the postmark on a letter unless we want to know the date, Manik-da's curiosity and attention to detail meant he would not only see the postmark, but it would also get etched in his memory forever.

If we move ahead to *Joi Baba Felunath*, were you under any kind of pressure when you played Feluda again, now that he had become Bengal's most loved icon?

Pressure is not the right word. I was excited surely but not tense. I was determined to ensure there was continuity between the two films and had prepared myself accordingly. For a man like Feluda, who uses his 'magajastro' (mind) more than anything else, you need to figure out how you use your expressions to win over the viewer. In my case, I used my eyes to do a lot of the job. Not always can Feluda have a frown on his forehead. That's why the use of the eyes. Think of the Calcutta Lodge scene in *Felunath*, where Feluda is trying to narrow down his list of suspects. As he paces the room with Topshe and Lalmohan-babu sitting on their respective beds, and states that Maganlal had not been able to lay his hands on the Ganesh, all he does is uses his eyes. These are the little things that I had done to Feluda as we moved from *Sonar Kella* to *Joi Baba Felunath*. The other important thing is that, in *Felunath*, Manik-da had given me a wig. By then my hairline had started to recede and it was essential to make sure Feluda did not age. Hence, the wig was the best call to hide my age.

Satyajit Ray and you shared a very special relationship. Tell us about the one aspect of his character that people know little about.

Manik-da hated self-pity. That's something I had always noticed. I will give you two examples to try and explain that. In *Felunath*, all of us had to climb a lot of stairs because a number of scenes were filmed in the palace of the rajas of Darbhanga. From the ghat, the stairs went straight up to the gates of the palace. There is the one scene where Feluda confirms his assumption that Machhli Baba is a fraud. He sees Machhli Baba taking a bath and decides to tail him to his hideout, which is at the very top of the stairs in the palace. I was still fairly fit and had climbed up the stairs without any trouble. On reaching the top, I realized that Manik-da, who had started to experience knee trouble, was finding it very difficult to climb the steep stairs. When he finally came up, it was apparent to me that he was in serious pain. But when I asked him, all he said was, '*Haan, hantu gulo to ar ager moto nei.*' (Ya, my knees are no longer the same.) It was clear he did not want to talk about it any further.

The other instance was the extraordinary last sequence of *Sonar Kella*. Had it been any other director, he would have asked us to stay on for a couple of days to finish the shoot. Not Manik-da. When he realized that I had to go back to Kolkata, not for a moment did he think of asking me to extend my stay. Rather, by doing what he did on the last day, he encouraged every member of the unit to surpass themselves. This ability of his to lead from the front made the task of working with Manik-da that much more special.

After *Joi Baba Felunath* did you not want to play Feluda? I have heard that Bibhas Chakrabarty, who did Feluda for television, found it hard to convince you?

Yes, I was rather reluctant to play Feluda when Bibhas Chakrabarty approached me. It was for no other reason but age. I had lost a lot of hair by then, and had also started to put on a bit of weight. As far as I was concerned, I was not in the best physical shape to play Feluda, and I did not want to do injustice to the character. Also, I did not want to give people a chance to compare it with *Sonar Kella* and *Joi Baba Felunath* and say I was not good enough any more. Manik-da, however, wanted me to play Feluda, and had even told me so on more than one occasion. In one of our conversations when I complained to him about losing hair and suggested that was one of the reasons why I should not play Feluda, all he said was I should go back to using the wig he had designed for me during *Felunath*. That told me he wanted me to keep playing Feluda for the time being.

At the time you played Feluda, you were also an established romantic hero. But Feluda does not have a love interest. In fact, women don't seem to interest him at all. Nor does he ever think of getting married. Was that a problem for you?

No, it wasn't. I have always loved playing different kinds of characters and that's how I approached my work. Yes, the absence of women in Feluda stories is indeed a noticeable thing, but that was never something I was bothered about. Because Ray wanted Feluda to be read and watched by school-goers, he was conscious not to introduce women or romance into the ambit to the Feluda adventures. Some people have been critical of this but, personally, I never had any issue with it.

What about the two other Feluda's after you – Sabyasachi Chakrabarty and Abir Chatterjee? What's your take on them? Do you think they have done justice to the character?

People have enjoyed watching them and I think both of them are very talented actors. Sabyasachi, who played Feluda after me, had a great voice and also had the physique to play the character. I remember speaking to him on occasions about Feluda. The one thing he did not do to start with was use his eyes. Because he always wore spectacles, it would anyway be more difficult for him to use his eyes better. However, in the later films, I was impressed to see him use his eyes more. That made him a much better Feluda.

Abir is a very good choice. He has the looks and the height to do justice to the character. Also, he comes from a theatre family, and it should not be difficult for him to grow into the character. Finally, he is at the perfect age to play Feluda. He can easily play the character for the next decade or so. I must confess I have not seen *Badshahi Angti* yet, but having seen some of Abir's other films and having worked with him on a couple of projects, I am optimistic about his success.

While we are talking about the men who have played Feluda, one should also remember that the great Shashi Kapoor played Feluda in the tele-series *Joto Kando Kathmandute*. Despite his presence, the series was not received particularly well. In fact, I remember meeting Manik-da the day after the first episode was broadcast. He too did not seem too enthused, and said he was apprehensive the Bengali audience would not take it well. If I think back to why this was the case, the most likely reason is Shashi Kapoor had put on a lot of weight. He had aged by the mid-1980s. Frankly, he was not the Feluda we knew from the stories. While to a non-Bengali audience it was okay, because they did not know

the books or the two Bengali films that preceded the tele-series, to
the discerning Bengali audience and Feluda fan, it was difficult to
appreciate *Joto Kando Kathmandute*.

**A word on Lalmohan-babu please. And here I am
referring specifically to Santosh Dutta. The success
of *Sonar Kella* and *Joi Baba Felunath* also owes to the
greatness of Santosh Dutta as an actor, doesn't it?**

Oh, of course. Santosh Dutta was absolutely brilliant. It is as if
the character of Lalmohan-babu was modelled after him. In fact, I
wouldn't be wrong if I say no one, and that includes Rabi Ghosh,
managed to do justice to Jatayu once Santosh Dutta had left the
scene. Bengali cinema has always had a history of great clowns or
men who could make their audience laugh. Take Bhanu Banerjee
or Jahar Ray, for example. They have acted in a lot of average or
even poor films. It is because of their individual brilliance that
these films turned watchable. Actors like Tulsi Chakraborty, Bhanu
Banerjee, Jahar Ray come once in a generation and the Bengali
film industry must consider it blessed that all of them worked in
the same era to enrich the industry. Santosh Dutta was of the same
calibre and class as some of these legends. His sense of humour,
wit, intelligence and subtle mannerisms made Lalmohan-babu
one of the most loved characters of all time. Had Santosh Dutta
not divided his time between his legal profession and films – he
was a reputed lawyer as you may know – he would have become a
legend in his own right. Utpal Dutta too was absolutely sensational
as Maganlal. Kanu Bandyopadhyay as Mandar Bose and Utpal
Dutta as Maganlal were absolutely critical to the success of *Sonar
Kella* and *Joi Baba Felunath*.

If there is one Feluda story that you would have wanted to see being made by Satyajit Ray, and one that you would have loved to be part of, which one would that be and why?

Kailashe Kelenkari. I would have loved to do *Kailashe Kelenkari* for the one simple reason that I mentioned earlier. Felu takes up the case on his own to ensure Indian national treasure is not siphoned off by a group of miscreants. That's what appealed to me a great deal. In fact, it is also why I personally like *Joi Baba Felunath* more than *Sonar Kella*. While *Sonar Kella* has its own romance, *Joi Baba Felunath* conveys a number of very important messages, which will always have lasting values in our lives.

Finally, as Feluda turns fifty, what do you think lies ahead for Ray's immortal creation? Do you think he is finally turning old?

There are some things that cannot happen. Feluda turning old is one of them. His fans across the world will not allow it to happen. I don't know what lies ahead for the franchise, but I can surely tell you I was privileged and fortunate to have played Ray's sleuth in my career. It made me universally acceptable across the spectrum of Bengali society, and for that reason I will be indebted to Feluda.

সন্দীপ রায়ের

RAMOJI
FILM CITY
PRESENTS

উষাকিরণ মুভিজ-এর
নিবেদন

বোম্বাইয়ের
বোম্বেটে

সত্যজিৎ রায়ের
কাহিনী অবলম্বনে
রামোজী রাও
প্রযোজিত

'In My Mind, I Was Feluda'

Boria Majumdar in Conversation with Sabyasachi Chakrabarty

Fans had almost given up hope there would be another Feluda film. Soumitra Chatterjee was too old to play the character, and Santosh Dutta was no more. But then, Sabyasachi Chakrabarty decided to relocate to Kolkata from Delhi, and even summoned the courage to go up to Satyajit Ray and suggest he wanted to play Feluda. Ray asked Chakrabarty to speak to his son Sandip instead, saying he had decided not to do a Prodosh Mitter adventure without his favourite Jatayu. The rest, as they say, is history.

Chakrabarty, with his baritone and build, standing a good 6'1" tall, was tailor-made to play the character when Sandip Ray finally mustered the pluck to make Feluda in 1995 on the occasion of the sleuth's thirtieth anniversary. 'Everything else in life has come to me but this is the one character I was desperate to play, and I kept reminding Babu-da to give me an opportunity,' says Chakrabarty as we settle down to talk over multiple cups of tea. There is no Srinath to serve the tea, but Chakrabarty is indeed wearing kurta-pyjama and smoking a cigarette as the conversation turns more and more fascinating. 'I was extremely nervous during *Baksha Rahasya*,' he says. 'That's the reason why I am always serious rather than trying to bring in the subtle sense of humour that is so integral to Feluda. This is something I consciously tried to change from the next film onwards, and if you see my later films, *Bombaiyer Bombete*, *Kailashe Kelenkari*, etc., you will see Feluda far more relaxed and at ease with himself.' Chakrabarty, who still plays Feluda on stage, but isn't sure how long he can continue to do so with age gradually showing on his face, attributes a lot of his success in his three-decade-long career as an actor to playing Feluda for close to two decades.

As a child you grew up in Delhi. When is it that you first heard of Feluda?

It was my father who first mentioned Feluda to me and the earliest Feluda adventure that I had read was not *Badshahi Angti* or *Sonar Kella* but *Gongtoke Gandogol*, first published in 1971. In Delhi, *Sandesh* and subsequently *Desh*, where the adventures were published before they started to get published as books, were only available in the Gole Market area and that's where my father got them from. As a child I had grown up with Famous Five and Enid Blyton, and here was something that was far more interesting. I was hooked on Feluda from the first adventure itself. I loved the setting, the fact that the prose was easy and accessible, and that teenagers of my age could read and enjoy them on our own. Byomkesh was difficult to understand and enjoy. In that sense, Feluda brought in a whiff of fresh air in Bengali mystery writing. Sensing my enthusiasm, my father mentioned that there were a few more stories published earlier, and if I was interested, he could try and get those as well. I was delighted.

As a high-school student I had already started smoking and my brand was Charminar. In my subconscious, I was trying to be Feluda all the time – and the choice of the brand was a clear attempt to do that. Also, my friends often suggested to me that we should go and watch a film together, and invite a few girls with us to make it all the more interesting. Girls, inevitably, would put me off. I was firm I would not go for a film with girls. Rather, I preferred to be on my own, or go and watch a film with only my male friends. There was no girl in Feluda's life and I had to do the same. I was conscious never to allow a girl to come near me. In my mind, I was Feluda and was trying to do things like Feluda did. Finally, when I was in my late teens – and I must say by then I had started to break bricks and practise the nunchaku – my best friend and I started playing the role of the local vigilante. We hated eve-teasers and would wait to catch them and teach them a lesson or two. We would usually give them a few slaps and banish them from our vicinity with the threat that the next time the punishment would be far more severe. My sister, whom I hardly ever played with for the reasons mentioned above, was my bait in trying to play the neighbourhood saviour. Again, in my mind, trying to maintain order was something Feluda would have done. Only when we realized that we were being extremely childish did we stop playing the moral police.

Most interesting. So when and where did you watch *Sonar Kella* and what impact did the film have on you?

Interesting you ask this. I first watched *Sonar Kella* in Delhi with my family. Again, it was father who revealed to us all that the film had been released and suggested that we go and watch it as a family. I was in college by then and was excited at the prospect of watching Feluda on the big screen. I loved *Sonar Kella*. I loved the way Soumitra Chatterjee played the character, and it has stayed with me since. I loved Jatayu, and the Jaisalmer setting was just dazzling. *Sonar Kella* was released in 1974, just a year before the iconic *Sholay*. By then Mr Bachchan was already a huge star, and his mannerisms and way of dressing – loose boot-cut trousers, short denim jacket, long hair – had become a craze with men our age. I was also smitten by the Bachchan phenomenon until I watched Feluda, who provoked a serious rethink. Father too had once asked me why I was wearing clothes of a particular kind, and pointed out that the style would inevitably change in a matter of months. Would I yet again change the way I dressed to keep up with the fashion? Feluda, on the other hand, wore his kurta-pyjama and dressed like my father or grandfather dressed. This style had an element of continuity. As I result, I started wearing kurta-pyjama or the kurta with jeans like Feluda did, and decided not to change the way I dressed just for the heck of it.

I had also started to act by then and was involved in group theatre when all of a sudden my father passed away. I was barely twenty-six and faced with the responsibility of looking after my mother and running the family. That meant I had to decide whether to stay on in Delhi or go back to Kolkata. I had uncles and aunts in Kolkata, and Feluda as you know lived with Topshe's parents, having lost his own as a child. It was time to bid Delhi goodbye and go back to Kolkata. This decision was also prompted by the fact that my extended family was extremely supportive and offered all kinds of help in getting my career started. They could help me look for a job or get me involved in the family business if I went back to Kolkata. The decision had been made and Feluda had a role in it.

So how did acting happen? How did you get to realize your dream of playing Prodosh Mitter?

Once I was back in Kolkata, I was keen to join mejo pishi and pishemoshai (uncle and aunt), Chhanda and Jochhan Dastidar, and continue with my acting. Rather than wasting time at

Gariahat in the evening smoking and indulging in inane adda, this seemed a nice way to keep myself occupied. I had always wanted to do something creative. Then pishi and pishemoshai launched Sonex and started making *Tero Parban*. I was called one evening and was literally ordered to come the next morning with a suit and act in the serial. I had a solitary suit, tailored for my sister's wedding, and landed up in that the following morning, knowing very little of what I might be asked to do. That's when I was asked to play Gora, a character that literally changed the course of my life. People loved *Tero Parban* and Gora was an instant hit. Perhaps it was the very everyday nature of it that people liked to watch.

I loved playing Gora because in many ways he was similar to Feluda. He was upright, honest and was a man of integrity with serious social commitment. Also, up to a point he did not have any dealings with women. It was only after the serial had turned into a rage that women come into Gora's life. I did protest and said the character would lose steel as a result. However, it was explained to me that Gora needed to be involved with a woman. I was not convinced, but could do precious little because it was my job, which paid for my living expenses. However, I was not enthused by the idea that a woman would drop a handkerchief and Gora would pick it up to hand it back to her. I found it silly, and was gradually starting to get done with Gora. In my mind, Gora was Feluda and could not do silly things. He was imbued with a certain kind of maleness that was getting destroyed as a result of all that was being done to him.

Sensing my discomfort, and frustrated at my repeated protestations, I was given a very different role in my next serial, *Udanchandi*. I was the negative guy in *Udanchandi*, where Uttiya Raut played the hero. I was a wagon breaker, deliberately getting into fights and far removed from women. Again, this had the effect of bringing me closer to Feluda, and helped do away with the temporary disappointment of Gora getting caught up in the all-too-familiar web of the traditional Bengali family melodrama.

I was cast as the detective in my next foray in *Siddhartha Chatterjeer Antordhan*. Playing Somak Sen in this serial, I was gradually getting closer to Feluda. It may have been Somak Sen for the audience, but in my mind I was actually playing Feluda. Soon after my career as an actor on the small screen had taken off, I summoned the courage to meet Satyajit Ray in his house. I requested permission to make a serial using stories penned by him, his father and grandfather. I wanted to call it *Tin Purush*, and it was meant as a tribute to the Ray family. While Sukumar Ray and Upendrakishore Roychowdhury were no more, I needed permission from Satyajit Ray to be able to do the project. To my pleasant surprise, he said he had seen me act and needed time to think about the proposition. He asked me to come back later and do so after giving him a call. I did exactly as advised, expecting to be turned down. Ray, an obsessive perfectionist, would not want to see his stories made if he was the least bit unsure of the quality.

I was right. Ray suggested to me that quality of the work on Doordarshan was poor, and he wouldn't want his stories done for television. I decided to take one final chance and asked if I could shoot a pilot and show it to him for approval. It would not be for telecast and would only be done to show him and seek his approval. Once again, he said he would think about it and asked me to get in touch later. Just as I was about to leave, I asked Satyajit Ray if he would ever do a Feluda film again. He said no, not with Santosh Dutta no more. Ray felt that without a good Jatayu, Feluda would not work on the big screen. '*Shudhu ekta lok goendagiri kore jachchhe eta loker bhalo lagbe na. Santosh nei, ami ar* Feluda *korbo na.*' (One man just trying to solve case after case, people won't like it. Santosh is no more. I won't make another Feluda.) In my desperation, I suggested that there were others who could play Jatayu.

'Who?' Ray asked me.

'Rabi Ghosh,' I said.

'Rabi. *Na na*. Rabi Jatayu *korte parbe na. Tumi barang Babur* (Sandip Ray) *sathe katha bolo*,' (No, no. Rabi can't play Jatayu. You better talk to Babu,) he said, and stood up to show me to the door.

As we stood standing facing each other, he asked me my height. I said, 6'1", to which he replied saying he was 6'4". I said, 'I know, sir,' and made my way out. Since then I started chasing Babu-da, telling him every few days that he should keep me in mind whenever he decided to make Feluda. Finally, in 1995, Babuda decided to make *Baksha Rahasya* and asked me over to discuss the possibility of me playing Prodosh Mitter.

So did you have to give a formal screen test of sorts? Was your selection a foregone conclusion?

I was called to Babu-da's house and was somewhat surprised to see both Lolita Ray (Babu-da's wife) and Bijoya Ray (Satyajit Ray's wife) present there. Sreedas, the well-known make-up artist, was also there, and Babu-da asked him to do up my eyes. I have very few eyelashes on my lower lid, and in general my eyelashes are poor. To play Feluda I needed to do up my eyes to have a lasting impression on the audience. Once Sreedas was done, Babu-da asked Bijoya Ray for her opinion. She said, '*Bhaloi toh lagchhe*.' That sent an electric signal through my veins. I asked myself, 'Does that mean I have passed the test?' It actually did, and soon Babu-da handed me the script for *Baksha Rahasya* and asked me to go over it a few times before I met him next. I was visibly nervous. Much as I had wanted to play Feluda, I knew it would be the most challenging role of my career. A comparison with Soumitra Chatterjee was inevitable, and that was enough to put serious pressure on anyone. Babu-da must have anticipated my state of mind, and said that I should not watch *Sonar Kella* or *Joi Baba Felunath* any more. All I needed to do was read the script, and if I wanted to do more, he advised me to go back and read the original novel and look at the illustrations carefully. There were many illustrations of Feluda in the novel. He said *Sonar Kella* and *Joi Baba Felunath* had been made by another film-maker, and in them Feluda was played by a different actor. He may not be as good as his father, but between him and me, we would make an honest effort to do the film well. It was heartening to see Babu-da show such faith, and thereafter, mentally, I started to imagine myself as Feluda.

Did you meet Soumitra Chatterjee before you played Feluda in *Baksha Rahasya*?

Yes, I did. And he was extremely encouraging. He said he was delighted to hear I had been offered the role and that he had always felt I was the right person to play the character. When I asked him for advice, all he said was I needed to use my eyes well. He explained in great detail what he meant, and I must concede it was invaluable advice coming from a person of his calibre.

Tell me about *Baksha Rahasya*. How did it all turn out in the end?

There is little doubt I was nervous, and *Baksha Rahasya* was not my best performance as Feluda. If you see the sequence where Feluda tells Lalmohan-babu that the hotel is Clarks, the place is Shimla and the country is Bharatbarsha to pre-empt him from screaming out Swit-zer-land (which he does irrespective), you will feel Feluda is trying to lecture Jatayu. Again, in the car, on the way to Shimla, when Lalmohan-babu is speaking about how a boomerang is used, Feluda corrects him in a teacher-like manner. That's not how it should be. Feluda never lectures Jatayu. Nor does he scold him. All he does is indulges Jatayu, who is no fool himself, because an unintelligent person cannot write twenty-eight thrillers, all best-sellers. I should have said these dialogues with a hint of a smile on my face. When I finally realized my error, it was too late to change. Babu-da had very little time at hand, and a retake wasn't a possibility. I said to myself that I would be far more relaxed from the next project onwards, and make sure that Felu shares many lighter moments with Jatayu. I consciously tried to do this when shooting for *Gosainpur Sargaram*, and if you see the later films you will see Feluda smiling a lot more.

The one scene in *Baksha Rahasya* that we were all looking forward to doing was the one in Shimla in the snow. Babu-da had done a recce, and we caught up with him in Delhi when he was on his way back. The first thing he said to us was that the Shimla shoot would be gorgeous with all the snow around. Snow in Bengali films was a rarity, and it was expected to work very well with the audience. However, when we finally reached Shimla, we were stunned to see that there was no trace of snow anywhere. The locals told us that, with the sun out in full force, all the snow had disappeared. Babu-da was upset at the sudden turn of events, but said nothing. The next day we filmed at Wild Flower Hall and finished the scene where Feluda returns the suitcase to Mr Dhameeja. Even while filming, we were hoping it would snow that night, and we could shoot the climax the next morning. It did not, and all we did the next day was film the scenes inside the hotel. Because we were operating on a tight budget, I really don't know what we would have done had it not snowed that night. Thankfully, the next morning, Shimla was all white. Babu-da was delighted, and we managed to shoot the film's climax to our satisfaction.

Tell me a little about Jatayu. When Sandip Ray tried to launch you as Feluda, he was also looking to relaunch Jatayu, which, everyone agrees, is one of the most difficult things to do if you are a Bengali film-maker?

Oh yes. Santosh Dutta as Jatayu was just fantastic. Satyajit Ray changed the whole character of Jatayu for him. And, like I said, it was because Santosh Dutta was no more that Satyajit Ray refused to do another Feluda film. So there is little doubt Babu-da had a very difficult job at hand.

However, I do think Rabi Ghosh was very good as Jatayu. It cannot be that a character is set in stone and no one else can play it. That's never happened anywhere else in the world and can't happen here as well. For example, Jeremy Brett was brilliant as Sherlock Holmes. That doesn't mean Benedict Cumberbatch can't do it better. Again, David Suchet is outstanding as Poirot. But does that mean no one else will ever do Hercule Poirot, and that the franchise is dead? Jatayu is no clown, and I thought Rabi Ghosh played the character extremely well in *Baksha Rahasya*. It is a pity that he passed away after doing *Gosainpur Sargaram*. Had he done a few more Feluda films, he would surely have found acceptance as Jatayu. Rabi Ghosh portrayed Jatayu as an intelligent man, and I would think the success of *Baksha Rahasya* owes a lot to his acceptance as the new Lalmohan-babu.

You went on to do a whopping eleven Feluda films in your career. Which is your favourite and why?

If I look back, I am proud to have been associated with so many Feluda adventures. In my three-decade-long career as an actor, every character that I have played has come to me. I have never asked a director for a particular role, excepting Feluda. This is the one character I was desperate to play and I remain grateful to Sandip Ray for giving me the opportunity. In fact, I am fairly certain that Satyajit Ray must have said something to his son about me. I have never asked Babu-da about this, but it is my hunch that Babu-da must have discussed the issue with his father. It is thanks to him that I continue to be Feluda to a generation of Bengalis. Some people used to know me as Gora-da, but later I was only Feluda.

It is very hard for me to pick a personal favourite. Each story has its uniqueness and I have thoroughly enjoyed doing them all. Having said that, the one story which has given me the most satisfaction is *Royal Bengal Rahasya*. This is because a large part of *Royal Bengal* was shot in the jungle, and as you know, I am an absolute wildlife fanatic. Each time I take a break, I go to the nearby jungle or safari, and I just love being in a natural setting. *Royal Bengal* was shot in three sets of jungles and that's the only reason why I would pick that movie over some of the others I have done.

What about Feluda's villains? Feluda stands out because each of his villains are heroes in their own right. Would you agree?

Absolutely. None of them are conventional villains. They all have their own unique selling points, and that's what makes them so entertaining. I would like to share something with you that I have never mentioned to anyone. Not even to Babu-da. I have been thinking about this for a while. Tell me, what if I request Babu-da to cast me as Maganlal Meghraj if he ever does *Joto Kando Kathmandute* for the big screen? Or for that matter *Golapi Mukta Rahasya*. Initially I was a tad apprehensive. I felt this would be doing injustice to the audience. Having played Feluda, how can I now play the villain? But then everything is possible in cinema. Take *Ambar Sen Antordhan Rahasya*. While I played Feluda in it, Soumitra Chatterjee played Ambar Sen. The audience thoroughly

enjoyed the film. If Soumitra can play Ambar Sen, there is no
reason why I can't play Maganlal Meghraj. I would love to say,
'*Ei mukta-ta toh amar chai,* Felu-babu, *se apni jai bolen na keno.*'
(I must have this pearl, Felu-babu, whatever you may say.) (Laughs.)

Maganlal is by far my favourite villain, and it would not be a
bad idea to end my association with the franchise by requesting
Babu-da to allow me to be Maganlal Meghraj!

**Not only have you played Feluda on the big screen, you
have also done Feluda for radio and also for the stage.
Tell me about the radio and stage experiences?**

I have thoroughly enjoyed doing Feluda for the stage. My son plays
Topshe in *Apsara Theatrer Mamla*, and I play Feluda. Knowing
that it is one story that can't be made for the big screen, Babu-da
had given us rights to stage it, and we have been doing it for seven
years now. We did make a few changes to the original story, but
nothing that would have an impact on the way Feluda is perceived.

In fact, I must confess I am starting to feel I can't do Feluda on
stage for too long either. Age is showing on my face, and I don't
want Feluda to look old. I love the character far too much, and
will never do something that will not go down well with Feluda's
fans the world over.

As for radio, all we have is the voice. We have to reach out to
the audience by using the voice and it was a very different kind
of challenge compared to television or the big screen. It was a
great experience to do the stories for *Sunday Suspense* on Radio
Mirchi. We went strictly by the original storyline, and I had two
extremely talented people with me to do the other characters.
While Mir, who is one of the most versatile of artists, did most of
the characters, Deep voiced for Topshe. Our editor, Richard, did
a wonderful job with all the sound effects and people still enjoy
listening to these episodes.

Now Abir Chatterjee has replaced you as Feluda. What's your take on him?

I think he is a very good choice for Feluda. He has the looks and the physique. However, the one thing that Abir lacks is dialogue delivery. He has that good-boy image. His father and mother have been part of the stage in Bengal for a long time, and Abir would have done well to spend a little time doing theatre before entering films. He did not do theatre at all and that's where he could have brushed up his dialogue delivery and learnt a trick or two from his father. Stage is like net practice before a big match. You can say the same thing in multiple ways and that's where the stage experience helps. Abir will surely learn with time, and dialogue delivery aside, I think he is by far the perfect choice to play Feluda in the next few years.

And what about opening Feluda up to multiple interpretations? Do you agree with Babu-da not giving up his control over the franchise?

Yes, I do. However, I also feel that at some point, you will have to open Feluda up to others. Babu-da won't live for ever and the question is, what after him? Will his son Souradip continue doing Feluda? Even if he does, there are only thirty-five stories and not all of them can be done for the big screen. There will sure come a time when all of the stories will have been exhausted. What will happen then? Will Feluda never be made again? Will children born some fifty years into the future not want to see Feluda being made in their time? Maybe for the time being Babu-da will not want to open up Feluda to others, but at some point it will have to be done.

For the moment though, I think Babu-da is right to protect the brand. Take Byomkesh, for example. Dibakar Banerjee's *Detective Byomkesh Bakshy!* is the best example of what can happen if a brand is suddenly made open to interpretation. It is entirely

Dibakar's interpretation, and has nothing to do with Sharadindu Bandyopadhyay's Byomkesh Bakshi. I am not saying it is bad. Not at all. In fact, I am staying away from making a moral judgement. All I am saying is that, while a film-maker is every bit entitled to his interpretation, I don't think the audience would want to see Feluda in a very different avatar from the way he is represented in the book. He is a very emotional thing for us in Bengal, and opening Feluda up might have an adverse impact on his fans. He is the only sleuth who has been able to reach out to children, and a child between ten and twelve would hate to see Feluda do something that he is not expected to do.

Why did you stop doing Feluda? Is it only because of age or is there any other reason to it?

Age and my paunch. As I said earlier, I love Feluda too much and would hate to see him being criticized. I was uncomfortable with a paunchy Feluda and said to Babu-da during *Royal Bengal Rahasya* that I thought it was time to retire. Babu-da, in fact, suggested that we could still do one or two more stories, but I said to him that at this age I wouldn't be able to do all that I need to reduce the paunch. Arduous physical exercise is beyond me, and it was best I gave way to someone younger and enterprising. I am absolutely convinced I had taken the right call. But maybe, as I said earlier, I might still get a chance to play Maganlal Meghraj one last time!

'Soumitra Chatterjee Will Forever Be the Original Feluda'

Boria Majumdar in Conversation with Abir Chatterjee

He is the new Feluda. Following on after Soumitra Chatterjee and Sabyasachi Chakrabarty, Abir Chatterjee stepped up to play Bengal's favourite detective in *Badshahi Angti*, which released on 19 December 2014. Director Sandip Ray says that Abir – who comes from a family of actors, and has played Byomkesh Bakshi in his very second film, after a debut in *Cross Connection* – was the obvious choice to play Feluda. Abir did well in *Badshahi Angti* and is now set to play the iconic sleuth for the next few years, and he will be keenly watched (and judged) by Bengalis everywhere. Here's the new Feluda on the challenges involved in playing the character, the experience so far and more.

I would think playing Feluda is the most challenging role of your career and also the most coveted. Your thoughts?

Absolutely. There is no doubt that every Bengali actor dreams of playing Feluda. I think Feluda will rank among the most loved

Bengalis of all time, and to play the man on screen is a privilege and an honour. But to tell you the truth, the possibility of me playing Feluda was in the pipeline for a long time. Benu-da (Sabyasachi Chakrabarty), when asked who should be the next Feluda after him, suggested my name. Thereafter, I had many meetings with Babu-da, and each time I thought I was getting closer. But each time, the discussion did not move beyond a few meetings. After a while, I managed to get the thought of playing Feluda out of my mind. I was playing Byomkesh in the interim, and had put my heart and soul into playing the character.

Feluda came back to my life suddenly. I had gone to Priya cinema in south Kolkata for a premiere, and just as I was coming down the stairs, Buni-di, Sandip Ray's wife, spotted me and said, '*Ami toh anek din dhorei* Babu *ke bolchhi tumi* Feluda *korte parbe.*' (I have been telling Babu for a long time that you are the right person to play Feluda.) I was taken aback to start with, but also delighted. Then Babu-da called me again and asked if I was ready for the opportunity. I remember saying to myself there was only one reason for me to refuse: if I was raving mad. I was added to the cast of Babu-da's *Ekhane Bhuter Bhoy*, a collection of short stories released in 2013, and from the very start of the assignment, I was trying to take on the mannerisms of the iconic Prodosh C. Mitter. At the sets of *Ekhane Bhuter Bhoy*, I remember telling Buni-di that I should be wearing a kurta-pajama, like Feluda would wear at home. My efforts had not escaped Babu-da's attention, who every now and then would just say 'hmm' as if to suggest he had not missed it. Finally, it was towards the middle of 2013 that Babu-da called me and said that he had decided to cast me as Feluda.

However, it was not until the end of the first shot in Lucknow that I really believed I was Feluda. Only when Babu-da said 'Okay' did I say to myself: It is finally happening!

Tell me about it...

Sourav (Das) who played Topshe and I had reached Lucknow a few days before the rest of the cast had assembled there. The first four days of the shoot involved just the two of us. Sourav and a few of the other unit members had taken the train while I had flown into Lucknow from Kolkata. Soon after I had landed, I met Babu-da at the Open Air Restaurant, where we later shot the lunch scene in the film. Lunch on arrival consisted of delectable tunday kabab, which meant my Lucknow initiation could not have been better. Sourav too had come by then, and after an initial round of discussion and planning, we decided to have a look around the city. I saw the Bhulbhulaiya with the help of a local guide. This had the effect of easing the tension a little and by evening we had settled down in our rooms, waiting for the shoot to start the next morning. If it was tunday kabab for lunch, it was grilled fish with vegetables for dinner, and I was in bed by 10.30 p.m. The next thing I remember was waking up sharp at 3.45 a.m. Generally, it takes me a few minutes to get into action mode. This day was different. I still had three hours and fifteen minutes to our call time scheduled for 7 a.m. I could easily have slept for two more hours, but knew it would be a futile effort. The script was on the table next to the bed, and I went through all of it in the course of the next hour. I was just flipping through it rather than reading each word, and it did not take much time. When I saw the first light of dawn, I told myself that, in two hours, I was to play Feluda. I could soon hear the sound of the morning azan and by 6.30 a.m. had showered and was down for breakfast in the restaurant. My mind was racing, and only some food in the system could help me calm down. All of us had a big breakfast, and I also clicked a selfie to send home to show folks how I looked as Feluda on the very first day. The reaction to the selfie was strange. No one said good or bad or anything. All I got back from home was: When is the shooting due to start? Clearly, they were as nervous and tense as I was.

The first scene was the one in a tonga on the narrow road between the Bada and Chhota Imambara. Topshe and I are thrown a chit with 'khub hunshiyar' (beware) written on it. It was an elaborate sequence. The two of us had to be on the tonga to which a richshaw had been attached permanently to facilitate the shoot. It had been welded to the tonga so that our head of videography, Shirsha Ray, and Babu-da could sit on the richshaw behind to film the scene. All of this had taken a little under an hour to prepare. Also, the scene was being shot in a very congested part of Lucknow, and that meant a number of retakes were likely. Three or four times, cars came in the way and instead of moving past, the drivers would just slow down and start watching the shoot. This meant we had to cut and redo the take. Finally, when the shot was complete, Babu-da wanted Shirsha-da to check it and give us a thumbs-up. When he did, Babu-da too decided to take a quick look and when he finally said 'Okay', I looked at Sourav with an expression on my face that I won't be able to replicate for you, and pressed his hand saying, 'Now you are Topshe and I am Feluda. It is finally happening.'

From Byomkesh to Feluda. The transition could not have been easy. How did you prepare to be Prodosh C. Mitter?

I must say Babu-da was there at every step to make matters easy for me. He had asked me not to see the earlier Feluda films, because it was important that I started fresh rather than trying to fit myself into Soumitra Chatterjee or Sabyasachi Chakrabarty's shoes. Like every Bengali on this planet, I had read all of the stories and, frankly, Feluda is so deeply internalized that we have all at some point in our lives tried to play the character. Dialogues like '*apnake to* cultivate *korte hochchhe moshai*' (Need to cultivate you, sir [Lalmohan-babu said this in *Sonar Kella*]) have almost become a part of our regular vocabulary. Once I was cast as Feluda, I tried to ensure I did not put on weight, for nothing could be more disastrous than a young Feluda showing a paunch! In real life, I did bowl a bit of off spin and it helped that I had played cricket. More than anything, I tried to discipline my mind and ensure I was in the zone. The positivity in Babu-da's unit made a huge difference and added much to my confidence. Each and every person was there to back me up, so there was never a dull moment through the three weeks of the shoot in Lucknow. This was the first time I was away for such a long time for a shoot since the birth of my daughter in early 2013, and initially I was apprehensive. But the team made sure I never felt depressed or homesick.

Having played Byomkesh in all of Anjan Dutta's Byomkesh adventures thus far, I can tell you that there are two fundamental differences between Byomkesh and Felu. And here I will restrict myself to *Badshahi Angti*. In this adventure Felu is still learning. He is young and dynamic, but is not yet a full-fledged detective. He may have great powers of deduction and may have read a great many detective novels, but he has never before handled a proper case. He still works for a bank, so investigating a crime is not yet his profession. All said and done, he is not the self-assured Feluda that we know him to be. Byomkesh, on the other hand, has been there and done that. He is confident, laid-back and knows he is very much in control. He has solved a number of crimes already and nothing seems to fluster him. He is far more mature than the Feluda of *Badshahi Angti* is. I kept this aspect in mind while approaching the character. For example, when Felu is asking Dr Srivastav questions about the angti's history, there is a look of surprised appreciation on the faces of Dhiru-kaka and the others present. And when Dhiru-kaka says that Felu is interrogating like a true detective, Felu actually breaks into a sheepish grin. It is as if he is a little embarrassed at the praise. This reaction will never happen again in Feluda mysteries. Post–*Badshahi Angti*, Felu is much more confident of himself and his abilities to solve a crime. He does not need anyone's endorsement, nor does he seek any.

The second difference is more pronounced. Feluda is physically far more active than Byomkesh ever was. If you see *Badshahi Angti*, you will see a conscious effort on my part to demonstrate this physical agility. When we first reach Dhiru-kaka's house in Lucknow and are about to enter his ground-floor drawing room, we needed to climb up a few stairs to do so. I made it a point to jump to the top of the stairs rather than climb them one by one. Again, when I am chasing the miscreant who has thrown the chit at us, I jump off the tonga and over a cart that comes in my way. Byomkesh would never do any of this and is far more composed and laid-back.

While we are speaking about this comparison, I want to highlight two very personal things. The first is Feluda is an aspiration for every Bengali. He is a kind of fantasy for us. What we can't, Feluda can. We can't solve mysteries, Feluda can. We don't know much about history, Feluda does. When we eat a lot, we end up putting on weight, while Feluda loves to eat but is in top physical shape. He is the much-loved Felu-*da*, while Byomkesh is always Byomkesh. Not many aspire to be Byomkesh who has even married the sister of one of his suspects. He is a top professional in every sense, but isn't the fantasy or romance that Feluda is.

Finally, I would like to tell you about one particular scene in *Badshahi Angti* where Felu is actually in Feluda mould, perhaps the only time he is in such mould in the film. This is when he is alone with Topshe in the room and is discussing who the possible culprit is while smoking a cigarette and wearing a kurta-pajama. Now that's exactly what Byomkesh wears and does most of the time. My challenge was how to make the two scenes different? In this scene, I couldn't be more physically active like in the rest of the film. Hence I decided to try and smoke the cigarette a little differently and also create a kind of 'tribhuj' (a frown) on Feluda's forehead. This is a Feluda trademark and in later stories Topshe even comments that Feluda's tribhuj tends to grow deeper as he gets closer to solving the case.

Moving on, tell me a little more about the Lucknow experience: the food, people, culture and the experience of the shoot?

It was terrific. We were there for three weeks, and each day was an adventure. Shooting at the Imambara and the Residency was just unbelievable. But the first thing I must talk about is the food. We had the best gilouti and tunday kabab, and Roni-da (Rajatava Dutta who played Ganesh Guha) had a whole to-eat list in Lucknow. He would knock one particular delicacy off each day and would inevitably try and draw me into going out with him. After the first few days, I just refused to be drawn into his food escapades fearing I would put on weight.

Shooting in the most congested parts of Lucknow was a very special experience, and I must single out Shirsha-da for doing an incredible job. Some days, Shirsha-da had to shoot with a small camera because the crowd was such that it was impossible to use any elaborate equipment. He would drop a cigarette, and that was my cue to start the scene. There is one chase sequence where I am seen running through the most congested parts of Lucknow. While doing the scene, all Shirsha-da did was drop the cigarette, and as discussed, I immediately started running. Frankly, I don't even know how it got filmed in the middle of so much chaos.

At the very start of the shoot, like it always is with outdoor shoots, locals started to ask what film we were shooting. Some were disappointed to hear that there was no heroine in the film. At the cost of digressing, I must tell you that people always first ask who the lead lady is. This happens with Mr Bachchan's films as well. It is because people like seeing their fantasy women in real life.

When we were asked the name of the film, we did our best to explain what 'Badshahi Angti' (The Emperor's Ring) means. The name did not make an impact and after a point our local support team started saying that the name of the film was Lucknow Meri Jaan. This seemed to placate the crowd who thought it was a film on the rich history of Lucknow. But the real fun was still to come. Finally someone asked the name of the hero. One of our unit members said Abir, and walked off in a hurry. Abir was soon misinterpreted as Aamir and, in no time, we could see the crowd swelling. In fifteen minutes, a few thousand people had gathered and, after a point, the crowd had become so huge we had to cancel the shoot and go back. Shirsha-da and I went back the next day to finish the shot, and even before the locals could spread the word that we were back, we had wrapped up the scene and moved on.

From Lucknow, we went to Haridwar and the contrast was extraordinary. From the congested galis of Lucknow to the spread of Haridwar, I am confident viewers will agree it is a visual treat. And in Haridwar, the best part of the shoot was filming the evening arati. With thousands doing the 'Om Jai Jagadisha Hare' chants together, it was an unbelievable feeling. The rushes that we took during the evening arati in Haridwar can easily make a splendid documentary on the place.

Tell me about the reaction at home. How did your wife, Nandini, and other folks at home react to you being Feluda? And are things different for you on the roads now that *Badshahi Angti* is a success?

Everyone at home was tense to start with. It was Feluda after all, and all of us were apprehensive about how the scores of Feluda fans would react to me as Prodosh Mitter. So the first reaction when things started going well was one of relief. The feedback was positive and it meant I had passed the first test. However, to tell you the truth, it has still not fully dawned on me or my family that I am Feluda. A few weeks back, my family and I were returning home after watching a play and we were stuck at a traffic light. A young boy of five or six was looking at me. I could hear his father prodding him and telling him, '*Hyan hyan, etai* Feluda.' (Yes, yes, this is Feluda.) I looked at him and smiled, and he was embarrassed and turned his face away. Such things happen frequently these days, and it always feels good to be accepted as Feluda. And every time such an incident happens, Nandini, who has been with me since college, looks at me as if to say, 'You are Feluda!'

The one thing I am really intrigued by is how my daughter, who is now three, will react to her baba as Feluda. For her, Feluda is baba. Will that take anything away from her admiration of Feluda? Will Feluda continue to have the same superhuman qualities for her that we all have attributed to him? If Feluda does not have the same aura for her, I will be disappointed because she will be missing out on one of the best things in her growing-up years.

In all of this, however, I want to tell you something that I firmly believe. For me, Soumitra Chatterjee will forever be the original Feluda. I don't think this can ever change. Even after I have played Feluda, many others will do so in the future, and it may be that someone who plays the character twenty years down the line does it the best. Even then, this identity with Soumitra Chatterjee will not change. This is because *Sonar Kella* and *Joi Baba Felunath* were products of a unique combination when the creator of the character, Satyajit Ray, directed the films and cast one of the greatest actors of all time, Soumitra Chatterjee, to play the character. Some people may like Benu-da's rough-and-tough look the best, others might like my athleticism, but still, it will forever be Soumitra Chatterjee who is the original Feluda.

I have seen this happen with me in Byomkesh. At the time when I played Byomkesh on the big screen, people had not seen Sharadindu Bandyopadhyay's detective for a long time. Byomkesh had been done for television by Rajit Kapoor but nothing had happened on the big screen since Uttam Kumar played Byomkesh in Ray's *Chiriyakhana*. As a result, when Anjan-da cast me as Byomkesh, and because the films were received well, the first identity of Byomkesh has become synonymous with me. It is always challenging to upstage the original ... better to come to terms with this rather than feel upset about it.

So tell me, do you feel frustrated? Would you say these comparisons put pressure on you when you play the character?

Absolutely not. I must say I feel privileged that I have been chosen to play Feluda. I am aware that the brand is such it is always going to be bigger than the individual who plays it. Soumitra-jethu did not have this problem because in 1974 Feluda was not the icon he is now. As far as I am concerned, I think of it as an opportunity to play one of Bengal's most iconic characters. And as I have said to you, I am not in competition with Soumitra Chatterjee or Sabyasachi Chakrabarty. It is only natural that Feluda will be synonymous with the two of them for the longest time and I have no problems with that. All I want to do is play the character well and play Feluda for as long as I can.

What's your take on Byomkesh being made by multiple directors and in multiple languages, whereas Feluda is still confined to his home state? Do you not think the franchise should go beyond Bengal for it to be more widely acceptable?

I actually differ with you on this one. I am in agreement with what Sandip Ray has done, which is not to give away the rights and open Feluda up to a variety of interpretations. Take Dibakar Banerjee's *Byomkesh*, for example. It was entirely his take on the character and was far removed from Sharadindu Bandyopadhyay's novel. Now some people may like it and others may not. We in Bengal may have issues with it, having read Byomkesh in the original. But for the non-Bengali audience, it is perfectly fine for Dibakar to be taking some liberties with the character.

Take the more recent Benedict Cumberbatch's Sherlock Holmes series. I personally like it a lot. It is extremely well made and the research is extraordinary. While at one level it is far removed from Conan Doyle, at another it is very close to the original. The reception too has been mixed. As far as I am concerned, while I am watching Cumberbatch, I am agreeable to the maker taking a few liberties with Holmes. It is in a different language and that, more often than not, allows for a little extra liberty. For example, if I see Holmes smoking a cigar and not a pipe, I would not be crestfallen.

However, with Feluda it is entirely different. And here I speak as a Bengali and only as a Bengali. While many of us may not have been to London and may not have seen 221B Baker Street first-hand, almost all of us have been to spots Feluda frequents on a daily basis. We have travelled the same roads, eaten in the same restaurants and shopped at the same markets. We are far more closely associated with the character in that sense. We have grown up with him, know his mannerisms, his habits, his likes and dislikes. We know that Feluda will go to New Market to buy his regular supply of dalmuth. We have seen our parents and uncles eat the very same dalmuth that Feluda likes. Now if we suddenly see Feluda move from dalmuth to a croissant, or getting off a Jaguar and not a taxi and using a fancy mobile phone, we will not be able to come to terms with these departures from the original. For us, Feluda can't do certain things. He just can't. He can't have a love interest, can't or will not drive a fancy car, use a fancy phone and the like. If the franchise is opened up, I am sure all or some of these things will happen. People will take liberties with the character. As a Bengali, I don't want that to happen and support what Babu-da has done in the matter.

Now that you have played Feluda, do you think other directors are likely to be more accepting of you? Or would you say people will find it difficult to cast you now that you have a certain identity attached to you?

Thankfully that hasn't happened. I was seriously worried about this. As a professional actor, I want to act in all kinds of films and try out a variety of roles. I can't survive as an actor by only playing Feluda or Byomkesh. What I find interesting is that some of the directors who have signed me on have kept reference points in their films. For example, in my last film *Jomer Raja Dilo Bor*, the director Abir Sengupta kept a number of reference points, which could only be there because I had played Feluda and Byomkesh. What I mean is there are veiled references to Feluda or Byomkesh characters which are now associated with me and the viewer finds easy to identify with. On the other hand, there are others like Kaushik Ganguly who has cast me in roles that are totally removed from Feluda. In fact, Kaushik-da mentioned to me while we were shooting for his last film that he had deliberately created a role for me that was different. He said people would forget I had played Feluda when they see me in his film.

Speaking as an industry insider, I think viewers should watch all kinds of films. When someone comes up to me and says he or she is waiting for the next Feluda, I say to them that I am waiting for it as well. But that doesn't mean they would not see any of the other films in the interim. For if that happens, there will come a day when neither Feluda nor Byomkesh will be made. We need the industry to evolve, and for that to happen, we need viewers to watch all kinds of films.

So looking ahead, where do you think you need to improve as Prodosh Mitter?

I want to improve in everything that I do. Unless you want to get better, a creative pursuit can never reach the height you want to take it to. I am aware that I have just done one Feluda film so far, and there is a lot more that I need to do to touch a chord with the diehard Feluda fans. I am fully aware of Feluda's reputation and will do everything possible to match people's expectations of me. In a sense, the more difficult thing is behind me. The initiation is always the most difficult. I now know people have taken to me as Feluda just like they had taken to me as Byomkesh. I have done a Feluda film without Lalmohan-babu, something that I was always apprehensive about. Such is the aura of the character that to do a film without him was really quite scary.

Radio Mirchi had done a Feluda retrospective a few months earlier to commemorate the fiftieth anniversary, and had shown all the Feluda films on the big screen. When *Sonar Kella* was being shown, the kind of cat calls that I heard in the auditorium was just unbelievable. And it reached a crescendo when Jatayu came on the scene. The moment he started saying '*Bahut ho gaya, jyada ho gaya*', the entire auditorium started to shriek and shout in delight. So much so I could not hear a single word of the entire scene that followed. While the film was on, I even messaged my friend Rishi who is now in Mumbai and is an ardent Feluda fan that I was watching *Sonar Kella* on the big screen. All I wrote was '*Sonar Kella, bodo porda*, Ram Deora'. Within seconds, he wrote back, 'Prakhar Rudra, thai thai thai thai thai.' And his final bbm said, 'I hope you now know what you have got yourself into.'

So to be able to do a Feluda film without Lalmohan-babu and achieve reasonable success with it has given me the confidence to go ahead and do quality work in the future.

Finally, Sandip Ray is planning a new Feluda adventure for the fiftieth anniversary. What has he discussed with you so far, and are you excited about your second foray as Prodosh Mitter when the legend is turning fifty?

(Laughs.) Who wouldn't be? Indeed I am. As I have said to you, I want to absorb and remember each moment while playing Feluda. I consider myself extremely fortunate to be playing the character. It is a kind of dream come true, and I will do all I can to try and do a good job. Also, you might call me lucky that within a year of my playing Feluda we have the fiftieth anniversary upon us. It is a huge occasion – as Babu-da says, he had never imagined that Feluda would turn into the cult figure that he has been. It is remarkable that his popularity keeps growing with each passing year. This cult only adds to my responsibility and determination. At the start of *Badshahi Angti*, Babu-da had told me that I was starting with a clean slate. He assured me that I did not have to think of the legacy of Soumitra Chatterjee and Sabyasachi Chakrabarty. That allowed me to portray Feluda in the way I wanted to. I'd like to continue on this path and add my own little bit to the aura of the character.

Part Four

Brand Feluda: The Way Forward

Boria Majumdar

At the time that I write this piece, friends who are part of the Bengali film industry tell me that Bengali films, even those with the biggest stars, are not doing the best at the box office. The industry is going through a lean patch. Collections have been poor (except for some of the films released during the festive Durga Puja season) and there tends to be a sharp drop in audience numbers after the first weekend. They say that there is a general sense of alarm within the industry. But there is one guaranteed exception: Feluda films. This is a dramatic turnaround from the mid-1990s when Sandip Ray was struggling to find a producer for a Feluda film. *Badshahi Angti*, Ray's last offering, actually picked up at the box office after a week of its release on 19 December 2014. With Christmas and New Year round the corner, many Feluda fans watched the movie as a family. Repeat viewing is still a norm for a Feluda film, and that makes the franchise one of the most sought-after in the Bengali film industry.

In West Bengal's highly charged political climate, where student politics threatens to throw the establishment into a tizzy every now and then, this eminently non-political of Bengalis (almost un-Bengali in that respect!) still holds enough attraction for filmgoers. A recent Feluda retrospective organized by Radio Mirchi at Priya cinema in south Kolkata is a case in point. Seven Feluda films were screened over a seven-day period, every show packed to capacity. There was a near stampede on the last day to see *Joi Baba Felunath*, and many who reached late could not be accommodated. As a result, the organizers were forced to organize a special screening at 8 a.m. a couple of days later to allow them another chance to watch the classic on the big screen. Close to 30 per cent of the audience who made it to Priya cinema during this whole week were students from either Jadavpur or Presidency University. This is interesting because these are two of the most politically charged universities in the country, once known for their fiery protests and agitations. That students of these institutions should flock to a Feluda retrospective is somewhat contradictory. Our master sleuth has never taken a political stand, although he began his professional career in the highly politicized Bengal of the 1960s. We don't know what Feluda's political leanings are and which party he votes for. Nor do we know if he was ever involved in politics in his days as a student. Yet he continues to find takers among all sections of Bengali society. In Lalmohan-babu's words, '*Apnake toh* cultivate *korte hochchhe moshai.*' (Need to cultivate you, sir.)

What is it about Feluda that keeps him from becoming dated? The answer just might be in the kind of 'Bengaliness' he embodies, one which is more rooted than even the political culture of Bengal.

Feluda was Ray's popular rendition of the renaissance man: intelligent, well read, intuitive, argumentative, but not verbose. He gets things done but is never unpleasant or rude. He means business but monetary gain is not the focus – a very Bengali trait. Above all, he is honest and socially committed. This is why he tells Maganlal in *Joi Baba Felunath*, '*Ami ghush ni na Maganlal-ji.*'

(I don't take bribes, Maganlal-ji.) But unlike Apu – Ray's other immortal creation and one who is partly in the same mould – Feluda is not fragile or unworldly. Apu is at odds with the world he lives in, a world not suited to a man of his sensitivity and ideals, a bit like Ray in real life, who was known to never have actualized his own commercial worth. Sandip Ray mentions this aspect of his father's character too: 'Baba started writing Feluda stories for *Sandesh* without knowing that Feluda would become really big. Later, when the publishers gave him his first cheque, he was pleasantly surprised. He didn't know he could make money by writing and that too by writing stories meant primarily for children. We later heard how Feluda had become popular among the grown-ups too. Everyone between the ages of eight and eighty had started reading the Feluda stories. In fact, Sunil Ganguly would first read Feluda before moving on to other stories, when they started coming out in *Desh.*'

Feluda, it must be stated, is clearly different from Apu in his world view. He is more a man of his times with a steely resolve. May be Satyajit Ray deliberately wanted to make him more worldly-wise seeing the commercial success of the novels. Every bit needing the money to make his films, Ray, at one point, had written to Marie Seton expressing concern about his declining bank balance. Writing in the aftermath of the failure of *Parash Pathar* at the box office, Ray had mentioned to Seton that if he could not continue making films, he would have to return to advertising. Feluda marked some sort of a progression for Ray. He is that perfect combination of renaissance values and modern-day combativeness. Feluda is every bit Bengali while simultaneously reversing a Bengali legacy that one has come to associate with the failures of post-Independence Bengal. Feluda, from his birth in the 1960s, is seemingly unaffected by the raging unemployment, lack of industry and overall spiralling stakes of brand Bengal.

He is the superman next door. That feel-good Bengaliness continues to be at the core of brand Feluda. These are not mere stories about solving mysteries, but also about enjoying the afternoon tea and chanachur, about going to new places and learning new things about them, about adventure that is not only thrilling but also motivating. He brings a sense of liberation from the everyday grind in troubled times.

As Feluda turns fifty, and as we celebrate the man and his exploits, the question is: what next? How long can he continue not using a smartphone, not having a laptop? How long can he solve mysteries without using Whatsapp, Facebook or Twitter? Can a child who is born twenty years later identify with someone who is a bit of a relic? What will they make of a character who visits Sidhu Jyatha rather than do a Google search? Yes, that is part of the charm, but for how long? For those of us who grew up in that other world, Feluda is a kind of throwback to a purer past, a time when our faculties had not been dimmed by technological progress.

Sandip Ray has plans to make five more Feluda stories in the next five years. It may be that we see *Nayan Rahasya*, *Chhinnamastar Abhishap*, *Londone Feluda*, *Gangtoke Gondogol* and *Robertsoner Ruby* filmed in the next few years. Maybe we will get a Double Feluda in 2016 to mark the fiftieth anniversary. And maybe Ray will try and cater to the NRI sections of Feluda's fans in *Londone Feluda*, a constituency he is very conscious of trying to keep happy. 'I keep getting requests from Feluda fans from across the world that I need to make Feluda travel more. *Londone Feluda* is the obvious choice. England has opened up a lot for Bengalis, and it would not be a bad idea for Prodosh Mitter to go to England in the next few years. Only, I need a good Jatayu before I do this,' he says.

Feluda comics are a hit among the next generation of fans, and perhaps Ray might want to consider an animation series to cater to his NRI constituency, at least until Prodosh Mitter is ready to leave Indian shores. A Feluda app to connect fans worldwide? Now that's an idea too. Without making changes to the stories themselves or the characters (both of which Ray is loath to do), there must be ways to market the brand better. Given Feluda's thirst for knowledge and his inquisitiveness, it is unlikely that he would not want to know more about newer modes of communication. To hear him say, '*Byaparta ar shudhui magajastro diye hobe na re,* Topshe, *ebare mone hochchhe amakeo kichhu notun jinisher sahajya nite hobe*' (The case cannot be solved with the half of brain power only, Topshe, I think this time half from some newer devices may be needed) wouldn't surprise the ardent Feluda fan. Although as dramatic a change as the Benedict Cumberbatch–Sherlock Holmes one just won't work with his audience either. It is a delicate balance: to evolve the brand while keeping it rooted in the original.

And that begs the question: what after Sandip Ray? Is one film a year good enough to keep Feluda relevant? What about when Feluda celebrates his centenary half a century later?

For the moment, though, it is celebration time. We mark the presence of one of our own in the global pantheon of sleuths. We look back at the man who emerged quietly on the scene with *Feludar Goendagiri* in 1965, and sometime in the 1970s became a constant in the lives of children growing up in Bengal. In a very personal way, and for all that Feluda has done to me and for me, this book is an attempt to add to the brand in the months and years to come.

The Feluda Case Files

Stories, Novels and Films

Story/Novel

S. No	Name	Story/ Novel	First published
1	Feludar Goendagiri	Story	*Sandesh*, December 1965– February 1966
2	Badshahi Angti	Novel	*Sandesh*, May 1966–May 1967
3	Kailash Choudhuryr Pathor	Story	*Sharadiya Sandesh*, 1967
4	Sheyal Debota Rahasya	Story	*Sandesh*, summer issue, May–June 1970
5	Gangtoke Gondogol	Novel	*Sharadiya Desh*, 1970
6	Sonar Kella	Novel	*Sharadiya Desh*, 1971
7	Baksha Rahasya	Novel	*Sharadiya Desh*, 1972
8	Samaddarer Chabi	Story	*Sharadiya Sandesh*, 1973
9	Kailashe Kelenkari	Novel	*Sharadiya Desh*, 1973
10	Royal Bengal Rahasya	Novel	*Sharadiya Desh*, 1974
11	Joi Baba Felunath	Novel	*Sharadiya Desh*, 1975
12	Ghurghutiyar Ghatona	Story	*Sharadiya Sandesh*, 1975
13	Bombaiyer Bombete	Novel	*Sharadiya Desh*, 1976
14	Gosainpur Sargaram	Novel	*Sharadiya Sandesh*, 1976

S. No	Name	Story/ Novel	First published
15	Gorosthane Sabdhan	Novel	*Sharadiya Desh*, 1977
16	Chhinnamastar Abhishap	Novel	*Sharadiya Desh*, 1978
17	Hatyapuri	Novel	*Sharadiya Desh*, 1979
18	Golokdham Rahasya	Story	*Sandesh*, May–August 1980
19	Joto Kando Kathmandute	Novel	*Sharadiya Desh*, 1980
20	Napoleoner Chithi	Story	*Sharadiya Sandesh*, 1981
21	Tintorettor Jishu	Novel	*Sharadiya Desh*, 1982
22	Ambar Sen Antordhan Rahasya	Story	*Anandamela*, May–June 983
23	Jahangirer Swarnamudra	Story	*Sharadiya Sandesh*, 1983
24	Ebar Kando Kedarnathe	Story	*Sharadiya Desh*, 1984
25	Bosepukure Khunkharapi	Story	*Sharadiya Sandesh*, 1985
26	Darjeeling Jomjamat	Story	*Sharadiya Desh*, 1986
27	Bhuswarga Bhoyonkar	Story	*Sharadiya Desh*, 1987
28	Apsara Theatrer Mamla	Story	*Sharadiya Sandesh*, 1987
29	Shakuntalar Kanthahaar	Story	*Sharadiya Desh*, 1988
30	Golapi Mukta Rahasya	Story	*Sharadiya Sandesh*, 1989
31	Londone Feluda	Story	*Sharadiya Desh*, 1989
32	Dr Munshir Diary	Story	*Sharadiya Sandesh*, 1990
33	Nayan Rahasya	Novel	*Sharadiya Desh*, 1990
34	Robertsoner Ruby	Novel	*Sharadiya Desh*, 1992
35	Indrajal Rahasya	Story	*Sandesh*, December 1995– February 1996

Films

S. No	Name of Film and Year	Director	Cast
1	Sonar Kella (1974)	Satyajit Ray	Soumitra Chatterjee, Siddhartha Chatterjee, Santosh Dutta, Kamu Mukherjee
2	Joi Baba Felunath (1979)	Satyajit Ray	Soumitra Chatterjee, Siddhartha Chatterjee, Santosh Dutta, Utpal Dutta

S. No	Name of Film and Year	Director	Cast
3	Baksha Rahasya (2001)	Sandip Ray	Sabyasachi Chakrabarty, Saswata Chatterjee, Rabi Ghosh
4	Bombaiyer Bombete (2003)	Sandip Ray	Sabyasachi Chakrabarty, Parambrata Chatterjee, Bibhu Bhattacharya
5	Kailashe Kelenkari (2007)	Sandip Ray	Sabyasachi Chakrabarty, Parambrata Chatterjee, Bibhu Bhattacharya
6	Tintorettor Jishu (2008)	Sandip Ray	Sabyasachi Chakrabarty, Parambrata Chatterjee, Bibhu Bhattacharya
7	Gorosthane Sabdhan (2010)	Sandip Ray	Sabyasachi Chakrabarty, Saheb Bhattacharya, Bibhu Bhattacharya
8	Royal Bengal Rahasya (2011)	Sandip Ray	Sabyasachi Chakrabarty, Saheb Bhattacharya, Bibhu Bhattacharya
9	Badshahi Angti (2014)	Sandip Ray	Abir Chatterjee, Sourav Das

Feluda on Television

- Satyajit Ray Presents, *Kissa Kathmandu Ka* (Hindi), starring Shashi Kapoor as Feluda, Doordarshan 1

- *Feluda 30* (Baksha Rahasya, Gosainpur Sargaram, Sheyal Debota Rahasya, Bosepukure Khunkharapi, Joto Kando Kathmandute for DD Bangla, later repeated in Tara Music)

- *Satyajiter Goppo* (Jahangirer Swarnamudra, Ghurghutiyar Ghatona, Golapi Mukta Rahasya, Ambar Sen Antordhan Rahasya for DD Bangla)

- *Satyajiter Priyo Golpo* (Dr Munshir Diary for ETV Bangla)

Acknowledgements

First, thanks are due to Sandip and Lolita Ray for opening up the family collection and giving me the many illustrations and pictures that we have used in the book. Babu-da and I spent endless hours discussing Feluda and these conversations have in a large measure contributed to making *Feluda@50*.

Soumitra Chatterjee, Sabyasachi Chakrabarty and Abir Chatterjee, the three Feludas, were all just a call away each time I was stuck. For the many hours with Soumitra-babu at his Golf Green residence, with Benu-da at his place and with Abir over many lunches at my own, I remain grateful to each of them.

Rajatava Dutta (Roni-da), one of my favourite actors, was a delight to talk to. He remains a common chord across many Feluda films and these conversations have immensely enriched *Feluda@50*.

To each of my contributors – Abhijit Bhaduri, Rochona Majumdar, Indrajit Hazra, Mir and Sovan Tarafder – I remain grateful. All of us are from the same brigade, the Feluda fan club, and I had real fun talking Feluda to each of them. Each of these essays has added much to the book.

Sharmistha, whose encouragement made me undertake the project. I can say little more about her that I haven't in the past in some of my other works. She is the driver behind most of my endeavours and I can only hope she continues to do so in the years to come.

To Aisha, my would-be two-year-old, I hope you start to admire Feluda in the very same way your father did as a child. It will add to your growing up in Kolkata.

Karthika, this is our eighth project together. Need I say more!

Finally, to the scores of Feluda fans who have helped in keeping the brand alive and will continue to do so in future.